SO LONG
AS THERE ARE
WOMEN

By Elula Perrin

SO LONG AS THERE ARE WOMEN
WOMEN PREFER WOMEN

Elula Perrin

SO LONG AS THERE ARE WOMEN

TRANSLATED FROM THE FRENCH
BY HAROLD J. SALEMSON

William Morrow and Company, Inc.
New York   1980

Copyright © 1978 by Éditions Ramsay

English translation copyright © 1980 by William Morrow and Company, Inc.

Originally published in France by Éditions Ramsay under the title *Tant Qu'il Y Aura Des Femmes.*

All rights reserved. No part of this book may be reproduced or utilized in any form or by any means, electronic or mechanical, including photocopying, recording or by any information storage and retrieval system, without permission in writing from the Publisher. Inquiries should be addressed to William Morrow and Company, Inc., 105 Madison Ave., New York, N. Y. 10016.

Library of Congress Cataloging in Publication Data

Perrin, Elula.
  So long as there are women.

  Translation of Tant qu'il y aura des femmes.
  1. Lesbians—France—Biography. I. Title.
HQ75.3.P4713   301.41'57'0922   79-26502
ISBN 0-688-03596-5

Printed in the United States of America.

First Edition

1 2 3 4 5 6 7 8 9 10

CONTENTS

"YOU DIRTY DYKE"	11
MADELEINE	18
DANY	43
JUDITH	68
SYLVIE	88
ANNE-MARIE	109
ÉLODIE	122
FRÉDÉRIQUE	143
VANINA	168
BEIJA FLOR	191

MADELEINE (Concluded)
   or, "When we are dead,
   our ashes will be together"
	208

AND YOU	212

SO LONG
AS THERE ARE
WOMEN

"YOU DIRTY DYKE"

Outside the Katmandou, the women's discotheque that I run in Paris, a taxi driver picked up one of my regular customers, to take her to her suburban home. Not a word was exchanged between them on the entire trip.

My pretty customer was ill-at-ease. But why?

Once he had dropped her at her door on a dark street on the outskirts of Choisy-le-Roi, collected his tip, and closed the car door, the driver, safe within his little cab, leaned out and yelled at her, "You dirty dyke!"

On his way back to town he may even have stopped to disinfect the back seat, for it had been polluted by "our kind."

A body he would never get to touch, thighs he would never get between, had soiled the immaculate back seat of his cab. Sure, the lesbian's money was good, but during the whole trip her presence was driving him out of his mind—his dirty little cocksman's mind.

Many of my customers get insulted that way—Isabelle was just one more on the list.

Is this the voice of a tolerant society? Is this what sexual liberation amounts to?

"Dirty little dyke!"

"Hey, there, butch!"

"Look at the cunt-lovers!"

"Go at it—down and dirty—you bitches!"

Can any one of us say that she has never been greeted with that kind of catcall?

I doubt it. That's the way we're treated. Or rather: the way we're mistreated.

Should we bow our heads and be silent? Should we just take it and go our way? Never!

But, then what? Shout? Strike back? Turn our bras into slingshots and take aim at the males? No, I think it's better to gnaw away at the problem patiently, eschewing rage or violence. As Madeleine says so well, in the first chapter of this book: First of all, we have to make men understand we are no loss to them, because they never did have any chance of winning; that we are wholly and permanently alien to them; that, so long as there are women, there will be women who prefer women.

Maybe it's because I'm one-quarter Vietnamese that I prefer smiling and waiting patiently, even when my heart is filled with rage. I think that persuasion is not accomplished through aggression, and that the constant drip of water will finally wear away the mountain, just as those thousands of patient little Asians, plodding along on foot, finally won out at Dien Bien Phu.

Kate Millett, in *Flying*, writes: "Lesbian . . . No word more terrifying, in my mother's mouth it is a snake hissing, Lesbian, intake of breath the unspeakable word."

But, Ms. Millett, it doesn't make me hold my breath. It isn't my lesbianism that causes me to be a feminist.

There are some women who become lesbians—that is, who begin sleeping with other women—for the same reason the National Liberation Front girls planted bombs in Algerian movie houses: out of political conviction, in order to make their protest meaningful through a decisive gesture.

But this is not necessary, either for women or for lesbians. On the contrary, I am convinced, it is disastrous. They give the world a totally false image of the lesbian, and they presume to speak in our name—but they are bisexuals, nothing but lesbians of opportunity, ostentatious and indecorous lesbians at best. And we are assumed to be like them, in filthy jeans and rumpled shirts, with flopping breasts and greasy hair. Once they have "become lesbians," they are relieved to think they will never again have to wear pretty clothes or curl their hair. Nonsense!

They come on strong, yelling at the opposition or slugging it out, as tough as karate black belts. Nonsense!

Even though the society we live in is patriarchal, conservative, withdrawn, monolithic, and repulsive to us as women, and even more so to us as lesbians, I think it is preferable for us to put up with it, to the extent that it allows us to live.

True, most men may be macho, cock-happy jocks, stubborn, narrow-minded, self-satisfied, and egocentric, yet I believe there are some tolerant ones among them, especially among the young. I think that eighteen-year-old lesbians will have a better chance than we did to live in a society in which they're no longer considered abnormal, but only of a different sexual preference.

Thank God (who else *is* there to thank?), the infamous yellow Star of David has been done away with, and blacks can now sit anywhere on the bus alongside white Americans. Maybe some day we lesbians will no longer be branded on our foreheads, molded deep in our hearts, with the flaming scarlet letter P for pervert, pariah, or other such epithets that society hurls at us—maybe then we will be seen for just the women we are, women to the womanth degree, women who prefer hyperwomen, lesbians in a word, proudly sporting a capital L, as in Lesbian, as in the love we have for another woman, this woman or that woman, the woman I love and the one who loves me.

I'm not bellicose; I don't fight. To be honest, I'm just flexing my muscles, trying to keep moving, just to live, live and nothing more. We are not trying to be Superwomen, or less-than-women. We just want to be, no more and no less, no better and no worse than any other— woman or man—just to exist fully within our difference, to share it perhaps, to fulfill it undoubtedly, and most surely to have it accepted.

The only task I have set myself—and I've no way of knowing whether I have the means or the strength necessary to carry it out—is to try to help my sisters in passion get over the wall that separates us from the rest of womankind. Once that barrier is gone, once we have been recognized as full-fledged women, we will be able to take our places in the front line alongside feminists like Gisèle Halimi or Benoîte Groult, alongside those Pasionarias who are fighting for legal abortions, equal pay for equal work, and, in a word, equal rights.

Only after we lesbians have been accepted for ourselves will we be able to take our place in the women's movement at large. That struggle is obviously our struggle, too, since it is the struggle of all women. But for the moment, my energy has to go elsewhere, to try to get us out of the morass of questionable sexuality into which we have been settled, shoved, and mired down.

I am often asked whether we are planning a separate lesbians' protest movement.

But what would we protest? What would we demand? Demands have to have tangible aims, based on concrete facts, to solve real problems.

Why would we want a separate lesbians' movement? To get special rights for ourselves? To be assured of certain privileges? The right to wear a pink star on our jacket lapels? The right to wear a little sailor hat with a ribbon around it reading GAY WOMEN, instead of S.S. MACHO, or what have you? But that would be foolish. If we were to create that kind of a movement, we'd set ourselves apart even further, build ourselves a ghetto, carry ostracism to its highest degree.

Each one of us is a separate, individual case.

A movement for our "rights" would make no sense, for no one can deprive us of the right to be homosexual.

What bothers us is the snarling hatred of some, the outrageous hypocrisy of others, which we have to overcome in our families, our careers, and our social lives.

"Spitting on the lesbian is forbidden." A lot of good it would do us if that were made into a law!

Our only demand is: "Leave us the hell alone. Let us love whomever we please."

But things are changing. Women see themselves less and less as being in competition with each other, more and more as all being in the same boat. And we lesbians, whose hearts by their very nature go out to women, just want to join the rest.

Why did I first spontaneously "come out" in print in *Women Prefer Women*? And what motivated me to do it? It was the fact that I was so irritated, so outraged, so upset, to see, to hear, to read things continually about gay men, without ever seeing the slightest mention of any lesbian. I had been waiting. Like the rest of us, I had been waiting for that woman writer, that fiery pamphleteer who might emerge as our spokeswoman, the one who would make us known as we are, and get us accepted.

But nothing. Sisters Anne that all of us were, we could see nothing coming. We were the *Arlésiennes* of sex, the girls with a guilty secret, the phantom tribe, the unknown, unknowable horde camping out, muddling through the maze of emotions.

Green pastures for the straights, blue skies for the faggots; but for us, just the blank space of *terra incognita*. Stop! Go no further! Beyond this line, there are only amazons (those women who perhaps have not even *one* breast!).

So I laid bare my heart, my sex, my sorrows and pleasures, my successes and defeats. I took this *one* woman who loves women and allowed her to be examined by the curious and the interested. Some understood this and took it for what it was worth. Others were not satisfied with it. My life was only *one* life among many, and the tree was keeping them from seeing the forest. What about the others, *all* those others? How had they come to be sexually inverted, how did they carry out their inversion, what did they make of it?

"You," I was repeatedly told, "cannot be considered typical in any way. You were too lucky, life was too good to you, your life is a bed of roses. But what about the others? How do they make out? How can they get by, living as lesbians?"

As Montesquieu wrote over 250 years ago, "What, you are a Persian? How extraordinary! How can one be a Persian?"

People ask for additional examples. Let the others tell their stories; let them come out, too.

"You have no right to say you don't like men, because you've only been intimate with one of them—but I've lived with ten."

"You didn't want children? You wanted to be a sterile fig tree? Well, I have two kids of my own."

"It's easy to be a lesbian when a person is comfortably situated the way you are. I have to work for a living, and I have trouble making ends meet."

"Lady Don Juan, you've spent your life loving beauty, and that's all you can get excited about. I'm just ordinary-looking, and have only loved ordinary-looking women, and yet my heart beats just as fast as yours."

All of these remarks, from different sources, were relevant; the criticisms were apposite. I had to reply.

The several lives I am about to reveal are not mine; they were told to me, entrusted to me, with the care people show when they're carrying a newborn babe or a very fragile vase: cautiously, at first, but with growing confidence.

So, here they are, these lesbian sisters: so different, so

diverse, yet all of their roads lead to the same Rome—Woman.

What a steep, tortuous, difficult road it can be, you shall see for yourself. Some of them are old acquaintances or friends. We have been following the same road for the past ten or twenty years, and their lives are as familiar to me as my own.

Others just spontaneously wrote to me.

Those who wanted it that way, I have allowed to speak for themselves; you'll hear their stories in their own words. For the others, I'll whisper to you what they confided to me or what I was able to gather as time and opportunity allowed, as their lives unfolded.

What we have here is a landscape, a landscape of women of varied backgrounds, ages, and love relationships; we have their tear-filled, joy-filled testimony, their tales of happiness and sadness, of pain and love.

First of all, there is Madeleine. She is a nurse at a hospital where she watches over 120 patients. She writes of her life, her long life of unfulfilled desires, her life so charged with silence and fragility.

MADELEINE

Brussels, July 12, 1977

Madame,
I just saw you on television . . . How can I tell you what it meant to me? What was stirred up in me, dredged up from my inner depths?

Would it sound pompous to tell you that now I can die happy and at peace because at last one lesbian woman has shown herself in broad daylight?

I am not young, madame. I am sixty-three, and believe me, it wasn't easy to be a lesbian back in 1938. I suffered —greatly. A whole lifetime of miseries, disappointments, and sufferings. My husband would rape me, and I had four daughters conceived in disgust and resignation whom I saw grow up and go away, to my chagrin, into the arms of men. I did not even have the consolation of giving birth to even one girl with the same sexual tastes as mine.

Thank you for being, madame. Thanks for having brought me this ray of sunlight before the end of my days.

I have ordered your book and am dying of impatience to read it. Believe me, madame, admiringly and gratefully yours,

Madeleine

Brussels, July 18

Dear Elula,
You don't mind if I call you that? After reading your life story, I feel as if we have become friends, and as though I ought to be able to call you by your first name.

How can I say what I feel about you? Before you, there

Madeleine

was only Nathalie Barney, whose life has been told so well by Jean Chalon. But Nathalie lived in luxury and ease. You had to struggle, you have had the kind of life that most women lead . . .

I don't envy you, but through you I have experienced all that I never lived myself.

My life was filled with the love of woman, but I was not as lucky as you, surely not as daring as you were, leading your life as a lesbian in the way you have.

I had not expected to get an answer from you. Or rather, I so intensely wanted one that I was afraid to be disappointed and preferred not to expect it. And you answered me so nicely, I felt you were so sincere in the empathy you expressed for me, that, if you permit, I will write you again.

Oh, I am not asking you to reply. I understand that you have plenty of other things to do. And, especially, you have to write for us again. Since you were listened to the first time, you will be listened to again, and you have to speak out about all of us, over and over again, so that never again will any woman be forced to lead the sad life I led, filled with wanting and unfulfilled dreams, so that a young lesbian who now starts in at nursing school need not be forced to hide her preference and her loves the way I had to. I, too, believe that we are born lesbians, and that we die of it in this hostile world. The life I lived was not one of happiness, but only a few petty pleasures: loves that were shared but never consummated, because of the taboos. I die over all those women I desired but could never have, over the ones I dared not approach, and those who turned me down and made fun of me. I die of the isolation, the solitude in which I live. My generation suffered. I was born during World War I, was a young woman during the next one, and then . . . Time had flown away, there were restrictions and pain . . . and then there was nothing left at all.

I love women so much I could give birth only to girls.

I would have wanted them to remain small, to be my dolls. I would have liked to keep them. But, one after the other, I had to let men come and take them away. And Lord, what a tragedy it is for a lesbian mother to lose her daughters that way, to see them going away, one by one. And now the joke is on me: All my grandchildren are boys.

Now I have nothing left. Only Death will want me, since women always rejected me. All through my life, I was denied the only love that could have allowed me to reach fulfillment: total feminine love.

Each time I wake up, I feel less and less able to continue on this lonely road. A wasted life, all of this love that I carried within me for so many years and will carry away with me to the cemetery in my village, out in the country, where there is nothing but the singing of birds to break the silence. My God, how terrified I am at the idea of being buried under a mass of earth, I who so love freedom, and the sun and the sea.

Oh, I'm not sorry that I'm a lesbian! I'm not sorry for what I am. I am only sorry that all my love was lost, wasted. I am so lonely. I exist for no one, not even for my daughters: They broke with me when they found out what I am. I no longer feel like living . . . and you're the only one I can say this to. If *you* don't understand me (and you are the only person I consider worthy of knowing my thoughts), then there will be nothing left for me indeed.

Every night, at midnight, I think of you. Often I wake up at five in the morning, the time when you are probably going home. And I feel like saying these very simple words to you: "Button up and don't catch cold."

I kiss you tenderly.

Madeleine

Madeleine

Brussels, July 28

... For so long I have wanted to tell my story. But what is there to tell? Nothing very exciting, because nothing was accomplished, nothing really done. I can't tell you of any earthshaking loves, only of a life overflowing with love.

And besides, I need to exist for you. You alone can help me survive by finally giving me the impression I'm talking to a person who understands me, who won't laugh at the fact that I can only love women, who won't go sneering behind my back because I looked at her too tenderly, gestured too fondly, one who knows how marvelous it is to love a woman and be loved by her.

You wrote how good it was to feel the body of another woman against one's own.

I realized then that I had never held Lucienne against me for a whole night . . . And when I phoned you (too early the other morning, I hope you've forgiven me, but I so wanted to hear your voice again and had not realized that to you noon was the break of day), I hung up, and thought of the fact that, while you were talking to me, there near you, in the warmth of your bed, there was your *amie* lying against you. I was almost envious of the happiness you shared. Oh! Take advantage of it, love each other, make the most of every second you have. If you knew what I would have given to live through just one of those sleeps of yours, to know just one of your awakenings, of your breakfasts together, of the coffee prepared for the woman one loves, the tray laid out with love, the light that you put out together at night . . .

When I was born, I hung on for dear life to the watch chain of the doctor who was delivering me from my mother's belly. Was it fear of being born? Or a first gesture of fond attachment? For all of my life was just one continual attachment. I don't know.

It was wartime. 1915, and the Spanish influenza was helping the cannons decimate humanity. I caught it. A German doctor saved my life, then a little later a British soldier cradled me in his arms . . .

The Charleroi–Brussels canal runs through my village. I used to like to walk along it, watching the barges slide along its smooth waters, dreaming of escape. And later, I transferred this love of the river to the sea, the North Sea. La Panne is my favorite beach there. I love the sea as I would a woman, because the sea is so truly woman—at times calm and reassuring, at others stormy and unleashed, never monotonous or boring.

My parents were simple people. Outside the house, they planted flowers. I adored flowers. I still like them. I was a great reader: Books could make me laugh aloud or weep bitter tears. My mother couldn't understand that: "Madeleine is too high-strung a child."

I wanted to go into a convent, to save souls. God did not allow it. I would doubtless have wrought havoc there.

So I decided I would save bodies. And I became a nurse, to fulfill my vocation.

I own a plot in perpetuity in my village cemetery. That way, I can be sure that I'll end up back home. I don't feel a need for a mausoleum; a simple cross is enough. What I want is to rest in the earth where I was born and where I lived my only happy years, when I was dreaming life before I knew what it was like. If, from time to time, one of my daughters should think of coming there and leaving some flowers, that's fine. I will be near my dear mother and the father I adored. There at last I will find peace—the peace I never found here in this world.

I wish I could tell you about beautiful tempestuous love affairs, but all I can give you is a life overflowing with love.

I am one of those who never had the good luck to bloom,

as roses do on a fine summer's morning. In all that I have to tell you, there is nothing truly lesbian. There is tenderness, friendship, everything that can develop, can come to count between two women, between any two women: the kind of complicity that can't exist between a man and a woman. I feel it all too well when my four daughters and I are together: Husbands and children no longer count at all. We are together like the five fingers of one hand: five women.

After grammar school, I was sent to a nearby village to study sewing. That was where I developed a deep friendship with Marcelle, a girl from my town whom I knew by sight. How we used to laugh together! How good it was! Sometimes we talked about love, and we would kiss each other on the mouth "to see what it was like." When I wanted to repeat what to me was more than just a game, she repulsed me. After a year or so, she started going out with boys. I was the alibi she gave to her mother. While she was doing her petting, I kept discreetly away, waiting, and each time I swore this time would be the last. But she was so amusing, so lively, and I enjoyed her company so much! . . .

She absolutely insisted on educating me. We secretly read *Lady Chatterley's Lover*. I thought the whole thing was really disgusting—but the young Lady on the cover was so awfully pretty . . .

One day, one of the boys in the bunch she hung out with, who was more daring than the others, tried to kiss me. I pushed him away and slapped him.

Finally, Marcelle got married, very young. I went on seeing her for quite a while, but something between us had snapped.

That was when I entered the nursing school at the hospital, on a live-in basis.

At the beginning, I was really not much of a nurse. I had to work very hard. I was trained by a woman—the one who taught me all about my profession, about the love for patients, about self-abnegation, and love. Just plain love.

Lucienne, who was older than I, was the supervisor.

There was no such thing as rest for us. By day or by night. After ten in the evening, nonregistered nurses were in charge of the night watch, and if at any time a patient took a turn for the worse, if a surgeon came in to operate, we had to get up, prep the patient for surgery, wait until it was time to return him to his bed, and then go and catch what rest we could until we came on duty again at six in the morning. Sometimes I rebelled against it. Lucienne taught me patience, abnegation, the love of the profession.

She was fifteen years older than I. She taught me what passion could be. But we never had a night together, not a whole night. Either she or I always had to be getting up. That was what I rebelled against. I think that during those three years when we loved each other and worked together, I slept very little—between working and loving . . .

If I was awakened to go to the bedside of a dying patient, when it was over I would take refuge in her bedroom. I needed the warmth of her arms to make me get over the tragedy I had just lived through down below. I had just witnessed death, and she was life.

What a wonderful life we had for those three years! We were living in isolation; I was alive only at the hospital, when I was with her. I forgot about my family; nothing mattered anymore, except her. Could a man and a woman have lived that way?

Then the war came. My parents were fleeing, but I refused to go along; I didn't want to leave Lucienne.

Marcelle had suspected what there was between us, and she didn't approve of it. We didn't really talk about it, because in those days people didn't talk about such things, but I could feel her disapproval.

That was when Lucienne almost got married. One of

her cousins died of puerperal fever, leaving a newborn baby, and her family tried to make her feel it was her duty to marry the widower . . . When she told me that, it was awful. I made the most terrible scene. I screamed, stormed, raged at her. And then I sobbed my heart out . . . She took me in her arms. We made love.

So she didn't marry her cousin's husband. But something in me had irremediably broken. My confidence in our love, my certainty that we would stay together all our lives . . .

Out of disillusionment, I let Joe, a friend of Marcelle's husband, take me out and make passes at me. Marcelle was delighted. I would finally be escaping from Lucienne's evil embraces. If she had only known! Her delight didn't last long when she saw what a catastrophe my marriage was and what it had turned me into . . .

When Lucienne had taught me how to make love, everything came naturally to me. I didn't need to learn how to make love to her. My hands and lips knew just where to go on her body. She had taken me into her bedroom, with her arm softly around my shoulders. I can still see her, taking off her nurse's coif, putting it on the chair . . . It all happened so easily, without embarrassment or shame . . . Never once did I ask myself whether what we were doing was right or wrong . . .

With Joe, it was nothing of the sort. What curiosity drove me to go with him to that hotel room, where he possessed me? I experienced neither pleasure nor disgust. All I thought was, is that all there is to it?

But I agreed to go again; I have no idea why. Three times in one month, and then it happened: I was pregnant.

I told the whole thing to Lucienne. She was a midwife, but she would not hear of aborting me. "We'll raise it together," she told me.

That was madness. I couldn't do a thing like that to my parents. And what about the hospital? Would they have kept on an unwed mother? I'd have been fired.

So, what to do? . . . I leaped into marriage the way people jump into the river . . . My God, what a hell it was! That man getting off on top of me, and all I wanted to do was scream! Eighteen years of repulsion . . . The minute he was finished, I would immediately get out of bed. He would snarl furiously at me. He felt that I didn't belong to him, but four times he got me pregnant. Each birth was an additional bond that imprisoned me all the more. How could I run away from four little girls, conceived in disgust and under duress, yet whom I love passionately? They were all I had to love.

I must say good-bye to you now, my unknown friend, who are nevertheless so dear and near to me. Take good care of yourself. I will call you next Tuesday. I have to hear your voice, before you go on vacation. With a tender kiss, your

Madeleine

Brussels, August 25

. . . I remember, it was the summer of 1942 when my mother-in-law found my girlhood diary in which I had recorded my tender love for Lucienne. She didn't know how to read, so she gave it to my husband, who read it. First he made fun of me, but then he got really mad. What a storm of insults! He tore up my notebook and threw it into the stove. He was wild with rage.

He had often beaten me before. Did I tell you that he was a brute and that, even in front of his mother or the children, he would often slap me because there was too much salt in the soup or his shirt had been scorched?

That day there were no holds barred. He came toward me, screaming, "You bitch, so that's why you lie there like a wooden board, huh? It's better making love to a woman, huh? You whore, you tramp, I ought to kill you, you lousy bitch, you hypocrite, you slob, unnatural mother, pervert, liar!"

What didn't he call me? He had taken off his belt and was hitting me with the buckle end. I crossed my arms in front of my face to protect myself, but not because I was ashamed. Oh, no, I wasn't ashamed of what I was, which until then I had hidden out of respect for him and because it was a well-buried past that belonged only to Lucienne and me. My head was aching from the blows I'd received, and I had backed up against the buffet. Then he started kicking me in the legs, and in the gut after he had knocked me down. I was crying out of rage and impotence. Now I was ashamed, ashamed for man, ashamed for woman, ashamed for love. How horrible it was to see such hatred for a past that didn't even belong to him. He was screaming with all the pride of the male at bay. I had my hands around my belly, because I hadn't had a period in three months, and I thought I was pregnant. I didn't say anything. But suddenly anything that had to do with him disgusted me. If he had planted another seed in my loveless belly, well, who cared? Let it die, let it be knocked out of me once and for all!

His mother was the one who got him to stop; he was tired from yelling and hitting so much.

I got back up after a moment. I wasn't even crying anymore. I thought I had used up all the tears I would ever have. I didn't know about the bottomless well, and that the tear ducts never run dry.

He immediately went out, still fuming.

I went and got my kids, and dressed them, and went out, too. Once in the street, I threw my wedding band down the sewer. The one I wear now is Mother's.

I went to her house. I didn't want to go back and live with this man who had meant nothing but hurt and misfortune to me.

But Mother talked me out of it. There were the two little girls, who weren't at fault. If I left him, and sued for divorce, I would surely lose them. And these two little girls were all I had left in the world. Lucienne had gotten married, too, to a very nice fellow. We see each other now and again, but very rarely. She has her life, and I have mine.

So, I went back to my husband. And he gave me two more kids. The first time he made love to me again after discovering my diary, he wanted to do it to me like a woman, to kiss me: "I can do that to you just as good as a dyke," he told me snickeringly. If I closed my eyes, for the slightest instant, I might imagine that it was a woman, and I almost got turned on a little. But there he was. Much too present, with his brutal awkwardness, his groans, his lappings, and making love now turned into an even worse punishment than it had been.

For eighteen long years, I lived through hell. I held on, held on, and then I just fell apart. I went into a depression. I was no longer able even to appreciate the beauty of a flower.

I was under a doctor's care for a year, and I told that doctor all about my life, except for my "unspeakable instincts." He did a real brainwashing job on me. "You have to go back to being a nurse," he assured me. "That's the only way out for you."

A law had finally just been passed that allowed a woman to go to work *without* requiring permission from her husband. For Joe didn't want me to work. I might have gotten away from him. He wanted to keep me sequestered, imprisoned, with my four little girls.

So I got a job at the Bordet Cancer Institute. I was going to be taking care of people worse off than I, seeing such troubles that mine would pale by comparison. And yet at the same time I revived, I came back to life in this hospital atmosphere, which had been the one in which I had known Lucienne and love.

It was tough. For two years, I got up at four in the morning and sometimes didn't get home till ten at night. Before leaving, or before going to bed, I had to get meals ready for Joe and the children. I had two days off a week, and those were put in doing laundry, housecleaning, and spending what time I could with my daughters.

I succeeded in putting a little money aside. My daughters had grown up. I sued for divorce after a more-violent-than-usual fracas, a battering that had left more marks on me than was customary. Marcelle helped me find a lawyer, and a small apartment in Brussels. She was all the more desperate at seeing how my life had turned out, for the fact that she was the one who had urged me to marry Joe. Maybe she held herself responsible, since she had wanted at all costs to fit me into the mold of normalcy. Anyway, she was there to lend me a hand and encourage me.

She was the one who had tried to open my eyes to Julia. But I hadn't wanted to understand at the time.

Julia was a beautiful Flemish girl with flaming red hair, a milky complexion, a few freckles around her long thin nose, Julia with the perfect face, the brilliant smile . . .

She came from Ostend. We lived across from one another. One day she started a conversation, in that cute Fleming accent she had when she spoke French. Both of us were pregnant, she with her second child, me with the third, and she asked what lying-in hospital I'd be using. We became thick as thieves, and turned into a sort of couple. Very quickly, we would clean our houses, make lunch, wash up, and then take off with the kids to the Parc du Cinquantenaire. In the evening, once the children were in bed, she'd leave her husband and come over to our place.

She helped me during my confinement, doing all the

things that Joe ought to have been doing. My little Angèle was sick with enteritis and also had rickets. There was a war on, but Julia moved heaven and earth to find rice and flour for her. We raised my little Angèle together, and between us we saved her.

I never mentioned Lucienne to her. Not once. I was too scared of losing what she gave me, which was everything, just everything. Except her body.

After Liberation, she had fits of sadness that I could never quite understand. She would stare at me the longest time, looking sad, then come over and kiss me tenderly on the cheek, saying, "When I'm near you, all my worries fly away."

There was nothing I could answer to that. I had to struggle to keep from taking her in my arms, as I could sense the aroma of her beautiful round white arms over my shoulders.

In 1948, Julia and her husband, who was a policeman, left for the Congo, and we moved to Charleroi.

I was back where I was born, but at the price of being separated from Julia. What grief that was for me!

She wrote to me. For the five years she was away, she wrote regularly to tell us how they were getting on. Joe put all of her letters into a file folder.

Finally, after five long years, she came back to Belgium. She lost no time in coming to our place, and she spent a week with us. Joe slept downstairs, on the couch, and she with me. That was the only time in my life when, for whole nights at a time, I felt a woman's body alongside mine. I waited for Julia to be asleep, then I would turn the bedside light back on again, and look at her. I would caress her with my eyes, listen to her slightly hoarse breathing, and want desperately to place my lips on her round shoulders, on her chest that heaved so slowly. Sometimes, a bit of saliva formed at the corner of her mouth, and I wanted to drink it in fervently. But I never dared make a move. I was too scared of losing everything by going after that "little bit more" that I dared not ask of her.

On the last day, Joe went upstairs to put away his bedclothes. Julia was still in bed. Suddenly, I heard the two of them, above me. I didn't want to believe my ears. I would have liked to tear them off so as not to have to hear. She and he were not concerned about the noise that they were making. So—Marcelle had been right all along when she had told me I ought to open my eyes . . .

When he came back down, I was like a madwoman. I was waiting for him at the foot of the stairs with a kitchen knife. I threw it at him. He ducked it, grabbed hold of me, and pinned me down, laughingly muttering, "So what? We both wanted what she had to give, and I was the one who got it!"

I was weeping tears of rage and despair. He had soiled everything, despoiled it all.

Julia came on down, luggage in hand, all ready to go. She didn't want to eat anything, or even to say good-bye to me. She took off for the station with Joe. And I never saw her again. Julia, my beautiful love, what ever became of her? Did she even suspect all the love that I felt for her?

Then there was Georges. He was a young Congolese who felt completely lost at the hospital, where he was interning. He was alone in Belgium and didn't have much money, just his scholarship, which was barely enough to get by on.

I took pity on him, then started to feel friendly, and finally affectionate. He was very sweet, with big sad eyes, very light-colored skin, a lively intelligence, and a good feel for diagnosis. He would make a good doctor. So I became his mother, his confidante, but he wanted more. He wanted my body. I lent it to him, out of sympathy, because he needed a woman, too. But I got no charge out of it.

Just as was the case with the husband whom I didn't love, this boy to whom my heart went out was not able to bring me to a climax, or even give me a feeling of well-being, of abandon, of complicity, which is the prelude to love. It made Georges very unhappy. He would have liked to satisfy me. He was very sweet, very patient, but in his arms I was just an inert body, unable to experience a thrill.

That was in 1955.

Since then, I have never made love. Or rather, since 1940 I have not known the consummation of love; and since 1955 my body has never again been close to another.

How hard it has been! What suffering, to desire so many women, their love, their kisses, and never kiss anything but emptiness.

Now I'm a shameless grandmother with white temples, but my heart has been used so little that it beats as it did at twenty when I see a woman I like: Françoise Fabian, for instance, my idol of screen and stage. I never miss a chance to see her! Once I went knocking at her dressing-room door, and I gave her a white woolen shawl that I had knitted for her. She was so human, so good! I kissed her hands. And in her next movie, she was wearing my shawl. How happy I was! She is the one that henceforth I carry around in my heart along with you, because she at least will never let me down, never hurt me, never laugh at my love, since she doesn't know who I am, since I'm just another earthworm among so many others, in love with my oh-so-beautiful star . . .

I know you are not in Paris, but just the same I let the phone ring at your place once in a while. That way, I have the feeling that I've been near you a little. With a very tender kiss. Your

Madeleine

Madeleine

Brussels, September 2

. . . After Julia, I was operated on for breast cancer. My body wasn't being put to much use, but just the same it made me unhappy to see it mutilated. A woman's body ought not to be spoiled. I hurt for the woman I was, not for myself, not for Madeleine. I hurt in the name of all those who, losing a breast, lose a part of their physical beauty. That was why I was so happy to go to work at Bordet.

Oh, Bordet! How that hospital and I became wedded to each other! I got night-nurse duty. I had twenty-four patients to watch over all by myself. And the things I saw! If I hadn't been sworn to professional confidentiality! I never sat down, except to watch over some woman in her death throes.

Sometimes we had as many as four deaths during a single night, in the whole building. We would lend each other a hand from one floor to another. It seemed like all the dying women waited for me to be there before they went. How many times I was to receive their one last smile as I came into their rooms! How many times I was called upon to close the eyes of a woman who died in my arms!

When the patient was young, it was a real personal tragedy to me. I'd scurry all over the place to find a flower to place near her corpse. Oh, yes, that hospital had possessed me, body and soul! I made love to it. I didn't care about days off, I stayed after hours. My daughters often enough threw that up to me . . .

We carried Geiger counters, for we were exposed to radiation from the radium bars that we handled. We night nurses had to remove the patients' vaginal radium between two and three o'clock in the morning. They got a tranquilizer half an hour before; then two of us would take them into a gynecological room.

I would take them in my arms. "Hang on to my neck," I would tell them, whether they were young or old. To me, all of them were women who were about to suffer, all on account of men. There were compresses thick with coagulated blood that had to be removed. I caressed their thighs while I tried to get the radium dose out as delicately as possible, for they were in great pain.

"How gently you do that," they would tell me.

One day, I was called in by the doctor in charge. I had been taking the maximum allowable time for the removal.

"You're too slow getting the radium out," he told me.

I got angry. "I'd like to see how you'd do it! There are all those bandages, and four or five compresses full of blood! And you want that yanked out of them without any consideration!"

He didn't like that at all. I was transferred—switched to the men's division. It was awful. I was leaving those sick women I was so attached to, and—even worse—I was leaving that terrific, wonderful Cecile.

Cecile . . . Oh, in the beginning, I could tell well enough it was all in fun. You know, Elula, a hospital is one of the most closed-off places there is, almost total isolation; and, just because of that, the ideal hotbed for festering growths! The two-facedness, the hidden passions, the petty scandals, all are like a concentrate of what goes on on the outside, a veritable microcosm.

And within that closed universe, I had already become marked as a lesbian. So Cecile, for fun and to amuse the others, made a pass at me. She was very nice and sweet to me. And, little by little, she fell into her own trap.

While we were changing a patient's sheets, we would rub against each other, our heads would touch; and when the patient's back was turned, I would dare a kiss that she would return.

In order to get into our uniforms, we had a small room with our lockers in it. Cecile would go there at the same time I did; but when she was undressing she would insist that I turn my back on her, while I stood there in my underclothes, dying to turn around, to take her in my arms, and hug her to me. I felt like the flame of such a tiny little candle, and my knees would be trembling.

It was impossible to carry on a real conversation at the hospital, so I asked her to come to my place for tea one day. We both had the same day off. She was married, but childless. So we arranged a tea date. I was ready an hour early: I had bought meringues, because I knew how she loved them. Ten times, I rearranged the cups and saucers on their doilies. I watched the clock, each stroke of its golden pendulum bringing closer the moment when I would at last get a chance to hug my beloved to me.

From the balcony, I saw her coming down the street—and then disappear. She must be coming up the stairs, just one flight. Fortunately. But she was taking so long! It seemed like forever. Perhaps she was out on the landing, blushing, not daring to ring? I went and opened the door: She wasn't there. I went back to the window. By now she was almost back to the corner. I ran down like a madwoman. I yelled to her, to keep her from getting on the streetcar, which I could see coming. But I was too late . . . I had to wait for the next car, which I took over to her place. She received me very coldly.

"I don't want to," she said.

"But why? Why?"

"I want to get ahead at Bordet. And with you, it would be impossible."

"No one needs to know."

"Everybody's laughing about it already. No, it's out of the question. Be satisfied to know I love you, but don't ask for anything more."

I went back home, my heart aching. I was sick for a week, crying, bleeding, unable to go back to work.

At the end of that week, I went back to Bordet, happy

at the idea that at least I'd be seeing her again. Better to see her, to gaze at her almost-gray eyes that laughed so, at the wisps of her blond hair that from time to time slipped out under her coif; better to be able to admire her dainty neck, her sensuous smile, than not to see her at all.

But I was in for a nasty surprise. Because I had been out so long, I found I had been assigned to another ward. I would no longer be working under Cecile's supervision. How I suffered, oh, Lord, how that hurt! In the morning, I'd sneak in quickly to put a flower or two on her desk, only to see later that they'd been thrown in the wastebasket. She wouldn't even talk to me anymore. She grew colder and colder, more and more hostile. What was it she had against me? Was it my shy, humble love, that little violet that only asked to be allowed to live in her shadow? Or else what was it she had against herself? The fact that she had been tempted to set out on an abnormal course? How could I know, when she didn't see me anymore, when I had become transparent to her, like my tears? . . .

Oh, cruel Cecile, in spite of everything, it hurt when I was transferred over to the men's building, for now I would no longer even be able to gaze at you in silence . . .

Fortunately, there was Annie. But that's another story, my very dear, very tender friend, and I can't impose on you any longer today.

Tomorrow, I'm going to take a train to Ostend to go and visit an old head nurse, and see the sea. The sea at least always took me into her arms when I bathed in her. I'll send you a card, because I only feel alive when I am thinking of you. Your

Madeleine

Brussels, September 12

. . . As I was telling you, right after that there was Annie. That was a case of love at first sight. She looked kind of boyish; she was tall, dark, with an energetic face.

For two years, I worked my way toward her. I would rub against her, give her light caresses on the arm; and she would let me, making out as if she didn't notice. When I saw her come into a room, it aroused me. I waited for her eyes to meet mine, worrying over that moment and yet yearning for it with all my being; and when it happened, I would melt away . . .

After the two years, on New Year's Day, there was a little party on the floor. At one point, some glasses had to be fetched out of the doctor's office. She and I went after them together. I closed the door behind us, put my arms around her, and gently kissed her lips. She did not fight me off, but let me kiss her, and then suddenly walked out and slammed the door.

The next day, I screwed up enough courage to ask her, "Why did you suddenly get angry, last night, after the—after we were together in the office?"

Her head was down and she pretended to be very carefully sorting some needles.

"I like you very much, Madeleine," she said, "and I don't like to have to hurt you. But, you must understand, nothing can come of this."

I was speechless, unable to eat or drink, unable to sleep at night. She talked to me less and less often, then suddenly one day introduced her fiancé to me—although she had never before mentioned his existence.

Had she dreamt him up as a way out of her own disarray?

I thought about killing myself. For the first time in my life. Like you, I hate the idea of suicide, I find it cowardly. But, as you have said, it's a good way to bring back the one who caused you to despair—or at least to try to. I was afraid she was going to go off on the wrong track. I felt she was so very much like me. I should have forced her, like a deer, made her realize her own nature. But then I could see again the look of horror that came over her when I had told her that I loved her. I just didn't have the guts to fight by myself against this being I adored but whom I perhaps horrified.

I was so upset that I went to pieces in the arms of Lydia, my second daughter, who is also a nurse. I confessed everything to her. And told her how I wanted out of this life of mine that was nothing but setbacks and sufferings. She consoled me. She was wonderful.

"Don't give up hope," she told me. "Maybe you'll finally find that woman you need. But in the meantime, don't do anything foolish. I need you."

"But you hardly ever see me. You never come over."

"I have to live my own life, Mother, but I still have to know that you are there."

How selfish children can be!

After baring my soul to Lydia, I felt I had to tell my other girls, too. To two of them, I immediately lost my martyr's halo. Before, I had been the heroine in their eyes: I was the exemplary mother who had been battered by her husband. But now they began to understand their father better. How could I get them to see how things really were? How could I explain to them the prisoner's life I had led? How would it have been possible for me to seek consolation and love from another woman? In order not to lose them, I had had to make do for eighteen years with mere tender friendships. And now my life was reaching its ebb, the sun was getting pale, and I had seen nothing, tasted nothing . . .

I've almost finished telling you this long sad tale of unrequited loves, this long funeral procession of tall dead young girls that I can see going by within my broken heart.

Should I add two or three more faded flowers that make up my personal herbarium, whereas yours must be overflowing with the pictures of beautiful living women who smile at you?

Madeleine

I think that, after Lucienne, I became an alien. People no longer speak the same tongue I do.

I've had some joys, each time my heart beat faster over some woman I liked. The joy of hoping—but then a love dawning was already a love lost and gone . . .

In my despair, I felt attracted toward all of the women that I came in contact with each day. In each of them, indeed, there was an element of joy. When I had to give up working, how empty everything around me seemed! Remember, I was always volunteering to work on New Year's Day, because that was the day when it was all right to kiss every one of the women . . .

There was also that little thing from Marseilles. I felt that with her something might come to pass: She was the one who arranged to get to work with me. I had drawn her to me and held her in my arms for a moment. She had consented, her body going along, pressed against me, but then she quickly drew back . . .

And another, also very young. But even though my hair was turning gray, my heart, every time it lit up with a new hope, would still beat a wild tattoo. This one put it this way: "I'm attracted to you, but there's no way. I live with my parents. So I don't even want to talk to you anymore. Keep away from me."

And that's that! They always understand what I want, but they're never ready to go through with it.

So why, how were you able to work out your emotional and physical life to suit your tastes?

And why do I meet all these rebuffs?

Every time I wake up, I feel less and less courageous. How I wish I were eighteen years old now! Just think, maybe soon, thanks to your fight, to your good words, women will be able to love each other without being ridiculed, persecuted by men. Because each one of us who follows her own instincts seems to them to be a prey that they're losing.

Get them to understand that, under any circumstances, we are alien to them right from the start, that we are no loss to them because they never did have any chance of winning. Find the words, help us to live, Elula; so that never again will any woman who can love only women be sacrificed the way I was.

Oh, if only this holocaust could make it so that someday some young Belgian nurse of eighteen, full of faith in life and ardor of heart, might be able to live happily while working at the profession she loves; then I'll feel that my wasted life won't have been entirely in vain.

I kiss you tenderly.

Your *Madeleine*

* * *

I could feel, from her last letters, her endless telephone calls, that Madeleine thought she was in love with me. That was unavoidable, for she lived in and through the dream of a life such as hers had not been. She projected so many things onto me, so much too much! All I could do was turn down the role she was giving me, and make her understand that.

She phoned me every evening. It got to be an obsession. What could I do? She wasn't asking for anything, she was asking for too much!

One evening she came to the discotheque. I recognized her immediately, tiny, with white hair, a smooth pink birthday-cake grandmother's face that you feel you ought to kiss and cherish. In a quiet slow voice, she said only two or three simple sentences:

"I'm Madeleine."

"I know."

"I came to see Françoise Fabian's play, and then to see you."

I had to react, to cut short her illusions, so that there might be a real friendship between us. I was very direct about it, as I always am, brutally frank.

"I understand . . . I understand . . ."

And I got up somewhat abruptly. It was a Friday; we were very crowded and I had a lot to do. I didn't come back to the bar for quite a long time. When I did get back, she was already gone.

In front of my door, when I got home, I found a bouquet of red roses that she had left there, probably during the course of the evening.

Was I cruel? I don't think so. This new passion of hers was to be nipped in the bud, because it could only end up by hurting her. I had preferred to make a clean surgical cut of it, rather than wait for the gangrene to set in.

Madeleine understood. Ever since, although she still writes me regularly, she phones me only once a week: on Tuesdays. And while she retains a tender feeling toward me, her hungry heart did not, like some female knight errant, build any new castles around my heart.

I saw her again a few months ago.

She came to my house "for tea." She petted my dog and my cat, showed me pictures of her daughters, all good-looking, blondes or brunettes, and of her grandsons. In her eyes, I've become that daughter she never had, the one who might have turned out to be like her, who, like her, might have had a heart that beat only for women.

Exit Madeleine, who loved women so, but all to no avail.

Madeleine is a quiet, tranquil stream, like the River Scheldt on which she lives, no uglier than most, in fact rather appealing in some of those prewar sepia snapshots.

Can one possibly conceive the hunger for women that

drove her all her life and is still driving her?

In one more act of sublimation, Madeleine, that little gray mouse, has made me her last sun, her final Venus, her ultimate universe.

That's Madeleine—resigned, self-effacing, afraid.

She probably sits and waits for word from me, in her little apartment with its potted plants and lace doilies, on the waxed pieces of furniture that she so meticulously rubs in order to make them gleam like the skins of all those women she has dreamt of caressing.

She must take a streetcar from time to time to go downtown, to walk in Rue Neuve or Place de l'Hôtel de Ville or even Galerie Louise in her beloved Brussels, where she keeps looking forward to my visit, even though she knows full well that I'll never come.

Then she'll go on home, on Waterloo Way. And on the streetcar she'll try to sit opposite a woman, because, if only for half an hour, if only for half a mile, she doesn't want to waste the chance to smile—perhaps to talk—to the only being she has missed during her entire life: a WOMAN.

DANY

"I'll end up thinking I look like a whore. Unless it's just the neighborhood: Ménilmontant isn't as classy as Neuilly. There are lots of *pieds-noirs*.* I got nothing against them, but when it comes to being macho, or out-and-out male chauvinist pigs, you can hardly beat 'em . . . So maybe the fact they know I'm a lesbian—which I've never hidden—turns them on, like hunting dogs that are spurred on by the toughness of the chase, or they may be excited by the prospect of a threesome in the sack . . .

"You know, men are always amazed that I don't jump at the chance when they offer to let me have their wives, signed, sealed, delivered, and ready for plucking. They think I ought to be delighted, and honored by the fact that they're lending their old lady to me, no matter how ugly she may be. After all, if she's good enough for them, they can't understand why I wouldn't be dying to make love to her. So they get sore, and resent me, and then—but only then—they start calling me a dirty dyke.

"For the working-class he-men in Belleville, lesbian and whore are one and the same."

* * *

Dany, the one speaking to me, runs a hairdressing salon in that picturesque district, with its many ethnic minorities.

After her apprenticeship in a shop on the exclusive Faubourg Saint-Honoré, her parents lent her some money to buy her first salon, and then a second. Now she has ten employees, her business is a success, and she keeps it running at top efficiency. Dany is a go-getter. She's the one I

---

* Algerian-born Frenchmen.

most feel like, in whom I recognize most of my own characteristics. The paths of our hearts and our loves have been parallel, so I have no difficulty in understanding and describing her life—always on the go, never depressed, ever buoyant and proud—qualities that help so much in overcoming barriers.

The barrier of homosexual ghettoization, the taboo of inversion, the love that dares not speak its name? Not for Dany. She is one who has never hidden her sexual preference; and the women who come to her salon, whether interested or just curious, always feel at ease in her young and pretty presence, with her direct, slightly boyish manner, and have their hair done without a second thought.

* * *

When I do lose customers (Dany goes on), it's their husbands' fault. They tell them, "Don't patronize those dykes." Yet, when I meet them with their wives, the husbands are all smiles and gallantry. They fall all over themselves snapping their fingers to try to hail a cab for me. While all I really feel like doing is to give them the finger! . . . Such stupid pricks!

And the next thing you know they're asking me if I wouldn't like a piece of their secretary.

I bumped into one of them one day at the corner café, where I was having a cup of coffee. Up to then I had only known him by sight. He came over and said to me, "Would you like me to bring my secretary to see you? She's willing."

"Oh, is she?" I said. "And what will you charge me?"

"What? I don't understand."

"Yes, what will you charge? Because, as I understand it, you're pimping for her, aren't you?"

And another one suggested, "My girl friend would really like to try it once with a woman. Come up to my place, and I'll fix the two of you up on the couch. You can put on the headphones, and for an hour I'll play you this unbelievable sexy music that'll really turn you on."

"Oh, fine," I told him. "The only thing that bothers me is, with the headphones on how'm I gonna be able to get my head up in your girl friend's crotch?"

How can you answer things like that except with equally ridiculous comments? Get angry and climb up on my high horse? I'm not the type for that.

Seventy percent of the women who come to the salon have never had an orgasm. That may seem unbelievable to you, but it's a fact. They tell me so themselves. Neither with their husbands nor with their lovers, even if they've had a hundred. Or, if they have had one, it's been by chance with one of them, in some unexpected position, or during a quickie, but they're one-shots that never get repeated . . . I think that they envy me. I look so happy, so well-satisfied, and they're not.

With us, when our affairs are over, we split. Without fuss, if possible. And later on, after a bit of time has gone by when we may have been upset, the storm has passed, things go back to normal, and we can become very good friends and go on seeing each other.

With couples who get divorced, it's not like that. There's always some wish for revenge, some grudge or rancor that is more or less conscious. And after both of them have remade their lives, they only very rarely go on having anything to do with each other, unless they're obliged to because of the fact that they have kids.

But we split up whenever love is dead.

But those women stay on. Out of cowardice? No, that's too harsh a word. For fear of the future rather, for fear or loneliness, fear of not finding someone else to share their life with. That's a worry we don't have and it doesn't play much of a part in our decision to split up. That's why I think that we lesbians are better balanced than straight women—because we're less worried about the future, and as a result are much more serene.

Of course, I'm talking mostly about the straight women who don't work, and are consequently totally dependent on their husbands.

* * *

Dany is right.

A few months ago, I went to a wonderful tea party at the home of an actress friend. There were ten or so women there: actresses, lawyers, newspaperwomen, broadcasters, decorators, some married, some single or divorced, but all active, amusing, attractive, and intelligent.

My friend and I were the only lesbians among them, but all of us had one thing in common: We were self-supporting women who weren't dependent on anyone else.

I listened to them talking, these women who lived with men, who loved men. And I was amazed to hear the aggressiveness with which they talked about them. They were the ones who were condemning the men for their shortcomings, not we lesbians. All of them described their mates as being unbearable and selfish. I must say that I, personally, have no special aggressiveness toward men; I am just indifferent to them. If they don't bother me, that's simply because of the fact that for me they just don't exist, or rather, they and I coexist, but we never cohabit . . .

Of course, I was listening with amazement, but also delight, to these women who live with men, who had absolutely no intention of becoming homosexual either out of any sort of conviction or even less out of natural bent. Their ideas about women and their unemancipated place in society were completely identical to mine.

These intelligent, assertive women had perceived and analyzed situations that I couldn't even imagine, for they were totally alien to me.

For example, one of them maintained that women who were financially independent could climax more completely than those who weren't.

That may be a startling assertion, but it does seem that sexuality is conditioned by the state of dependence. A woman who can get a new coat or five-burner kitchen range only through the goodwill of her husband often allows herself to be made love to, when her *provider* desires—not when *she* does. Whereas the woman who can buy herself everything she wants just on her own salary is more inclined to make love with the man she loves when and because she *feels* like it—without duress or prostitution; and since she'll be making love for her own pleasure, she'll make it better . . .

Dany had been lucky enough to acquire at a young age a profession that would allow her to make her own decisions in life, when she felt like it, and to get out of a marriage she had blundered into at seventeen.

What a crime to get married so young: to leave one's family in order to start one of one's own, without any transition, without a period of escape, going from one cage to the other, one prison to the other . . . But supposing my little friend Dany had had a baby right away, would she have been able to get out of it as easily as she did? How do you scale the high walls when you're carrying a papoose on your back? Just think of how many of our sisters were not so lucky and have had to stay locked up because of those dear little tousled heads, who are so innocent, yet in one way or another spell frustration in their mothers' lives!

Why had she gotten married? Because her parents found out she was sleeping with Philippe, and raised holy hell until he "did right" by their daughter.

Before him? Oh, there had been dating. She got her first

kiss at fifteen, at a party she went to. Apparently it wasn't Prince Charming's kiss, for now, eighteen years later, when she talks about it Dany makes a disgusted little face.

That kiss, of course, led to a lot of others, because that was the thing to do, because if you didn't who would invite you to their parties? All they were, were kisses exchanged during a slow, romantic dance, but they didn't go much further. Going all the way was not for her. She was a good little girl, even if she had fingers that were sometimes a bit too active (and effective!) when she dreamily fell asleep with lovemaking on her mind. It was a faceless love: Dany was not waiting for either Zorro or Barbarella. Philippe just happened to be handy at the propitious moment.

Why him? Just because, when you're seventeen, and all your girl friends are sleeping with their boyfriends, you do the same—peer pressure.

"It really wasn't terrific," she said. "Not terrific at all. It just seemed like stupid gymnastics, that I had to put up with. I didn't get a thing out of it. And since I don't know how to pretend, Philippe was well aware. He'd say, 'You'll see, it'll get better for you!' But it never did."

Once she had gotten married, and was a so-called grown-up, Dany was to meet and discover "the obstacle" only later, one night in a bar near the Opéra, where she went with her husband.

It was a blonde, a platinum blonde in fact, the typical Parisian cocktail-bar owner, almost to the point of caricature: forty-five years old, still beautiful, in full bloom, her ample bosom resting on the counter between two cocktail shakers. She leaned across the mahogany bar and told little Dany, "You're one I'd like to lay, and I'm going to."

Dany smiled. She had nothing especially against the idea, though nothing for it either. So, after all, why not?

The woman was beautiful, and she carried off her campaign with flair and dispatch.

Her apartment was upstairs of the bar. Dany came there to meet her after she got out of hairdressing school. It was five in the afternoon. The bar was open, but at that hour the barmaid could handle it by herself. The owner was upstairs waiting for Dany, in a white satin negligée, white mules, cigarette holder in her mouth, lights dimmed, and her studio bed covered in white satin. It was like a still out of an American romantic comedy of the fifties. Half-tempted to laugh at it, but still curious, Dany stayed on. The woman took her in her arms. And Dany liked her feminine aroma, the heady perfume warmed by her skin. She had a skillful mouth, and expert hands . . .

The first thing Dany was struck by was the softness of her breasts. That warm, unbelievably welcoming cushion that she could caress with her palms. There was nothing disconcerting about that. But what about the other woman's sex? Panic overtook her. It was the unknown, the abyss, the unexplored recess. As a little girl, Dany, like all the rest of us, had squatted over a mirror to spread herself, open out, peek inside . . . But what about the unplumbable, the mystery of that slightly wrinkled pink flower? Dany was worried. Dared she get near that sex, which was the same as her own? Suddenly it was present before her, opening to her fingers, and her lips. Would she know how to make love to it, caress it, bring it to satisfaction? She knew how to make Philippe come. But what about this unknown woman so like herself, whose lips were glued to her own? She decided to let herself go, let herself be guided by the impetuous woman who, for her part, seemed to know very well what she was about . . . An apt pupil, Dany learned her lesson well, and after a bit, she in turn put her arms around her friend and began to make love to her, quite well no doubt, for very quickly the room echoed with murmurs that soon turned into groans of delight.

Dany was happy. Not from any orgasm she had experienced, but from the one she had just been responsible for.

That's another thing that men don't readily understand, when in their determined pursuit of their ends they insist they "can do you just the way a woman does." They forget that sometimes there can be more pleasure in giving than in receiving. The enjoyment is not just in the arousal of the sex organs, but of all one's senses, hearing, sight, taste, and mind.

It's true that when you love, giving is the same as receiving.

No, it was not in the arms of the lady bar-owner that Dany experienced the apocalyptic thrill of the fairy tales. She had an infinitely sweet, diffused feeling, a kind of bath of voluptuousness, the tingling brought right up to the surface—at any rate, much more than with Philippe. But it still was not the true enjoyment of a climax.

After that, Dany's senses had been awakened, her mind was working overtime, and she started picking up young things her own age. Eighteen-year-olds, her fellow apprentices, or the girl friends of fellows who were friends of hers and her husband's.

She made out. She always made out. Dany was darling, with her sparkling dark eyes, her short curly hair, and her slacks that set off her tight little ass. The girls who came to her had never experienced a woman, but they were interested, curious, and in the end quite willing.

It was through the contact of these young bodies as inexperienced as her own that Dany discovered sexual enjoyment; through hesitating hands, and tentative lips.

Philippe considered himself a "liberated" man. He was not unaware that Dany was making love with women, but it didn't bother him significantly, especially since he could have her for himself whenever he wanted. And besides, he also liked to swing some himself, whether on his own or in a group.

One weekend, a couple they knew invited them to go out to a country inn with them. After dinner, and a few drinks, it was time to go up to bed. Dany was in her room, taking off her makeup, getting undressed, and finally getting into bed; Philippe in the meantime had not come back from their friends' room. Finally wondering what was up, Dany got up, put on a dressing gown, and went to knock on the neighbors' door. The wife opened it.

"C'm'on in," she said. "We were waiting for you."

The two men were lying naked in bed. The woman locked the door behind her.

"Get out of all that," she said.

Dany took off her robe, but kept her slip on. The other woman stripped down to her skin and slipped in between the two men. And then there they were, the four of them, like birds in a row in that wide king-size country bed: Dany, Philippe, the other woman, and her husband. Quite a foursome!

* * *

Philippe (Dany told me) started to touch the lady's breasts with one hand while keeping the other on his own thigh. Her husband was busy meanwhile twisting the dial of his transistor to try to find some suitable night music. To my left, I heard little muffled laughs. Philippe began to kiss the girl, and soon he needed both his hands to explore the territory. She let herself slide down completely, he got on top of her, and they began to rub against each other. Then I could feel them beginning to screw. I say "feel," because I wasn't watching them. My eyes were riveted on the sailboats that were crossing the bounding main on the wallpaper—but the sound I heard was not the wind in their sails! Philippe was humping her conscientiously. He's never impatient to get it over with, and he knows how to drag it out nice and long. I didn't feel anything one way or the other at the idea that he was fucking another woman. I wasn't in love with him, and I couldn't have cared less. In fact, I thought it was kind of funny to be in this new situation: I was about to look at them and perhaps enjoy what I'd be seeing, when her husband, vaulting over the two-backed beast, landed on top of my knees, his flagpole at attention, no mistaking what he intended to do next. I didn't so much as bat an eye, but hopped right out of the arena.

"No, sir," I said, "none of that."

"Why not? It's all in fun. No harm done."

"Forget it. Out of the question."

He took it like a gentleman, and didn't try to force me, but then he also got out of bed, grabbed his wife and pulled her out from under Philippe, the way you slide a mechanic out from under a car—by her legs.

"Come on," he said. "The game's called off. She won't play."

I was at the door by that time, slipping back into my robe, and heading back to our room, disgusted and nauseated.

When Philippe joined me in our own bed, he wanted to carry on from the point he had reached with his pal's wife. He was there beside me, absolutely determined to get his load off; it didn't matter what cunt he did it in. But I wasn't going to let him use me like that.

He was making an awful face: He was only half-finished. And I was making just as awful a face: I was disgusted with the whole business. It was shortly after that sordid episode that I met Elvire.

* * *

Elvire! I had known her, too, about fifteen years ago. Lord, how beautiful she was! Lord, what charm and what intelligence! How well I can understand that at nineteen little Dany was fascinated by her strange beauty, her feline ways, her hands that molded her sentences, underlined her words! Elvire, full of ambiguous sensuality that emanated from her boyish body.

From the day she met her, Dany never again slept with her husband. That beautiful, sensual, twenty-eight-year-old girl who had never known a man, who eliminated males entirely from her life and her bed, became her model, her ideal.

Their affair lasted only three months, but they were three decisive, lightninglike months for Dany.

Now Philippe no longer tolerated her behavior. He stormed at her: "Sleep with me to make *me* happy. I have a *right* to sleep with you!"

He went and complained to Dany's parents, telling them, "Your daughter is a dirty little dyke."

"Well, that may be your fault," they answered him in unison. "She wasn't that way before . . ."

Which served him right—and was pretty sharp.

Yet in spite of it all, because at nineteen in France a girl is still a minor, even though marriage may have given her certain adult rights, Dany agreed to go and see a psychiatrist, as her parents demanded.

She was very good about going. First he gave her half an hour to lie alone in the dark on the couch. Then he came in and asked her a bunch of questions that she answered any old way.

After that, he gave her a gynecological examination. (Can our lesbianism be measured by the length of the labia majora, or are there really still *doctors* who *believe* in overdeveloped clitorises due to excessive manipulation?)

He came out of the examining room to inform the waiting and respectful parents: "Your daughter is perfectly normal both physically and morally. I can assure you she is no homosexual."

So much for science!

Dany was soon smiling again: She had left her husband and gone to live with Lise, her latest love.

Or, to be more precise, her first love. For Elvire had been the flame, the fireworks, the brilliant burst of light that had illuminated her heart, made her recognize and accept herself for what she was. Elvire had been passion. But passion is not love. Elvire had been too exclusive, too total, too impatient to be willing to wait for her to get a divorce, to be willing to accept a woman who at night still slept in the same bed with a man, even if nothing took place in it. The very thought that Dany might either have to fight him off or get him off was more than she could take.

She was the one who introduced Lise to Dany.

Lise was thirty. Heavyset, squarish. Hair in disarray, with a lock that fell on her forehead which she was constantly pushing away so as to allow her incisive, clever eye to gauge you, form a lightning opinion of you. Lise was intelligence, charm, and culture. The minute she opened her mouth, she became beautiful. She was a newspaperwoman who was the mother of a baby, an eight-month-old little girl.

Dany fell for her. She went to live with Lise and the baby. Her future was beginning to show itself: Several other children were to take their place later in her life, always the others' children, never hers. For she never had any, and never wanted to have any, nor—deep in her heart or in her gut—does she have the resulting empty feeling that so many of us, myself as much as anyone else, sometimes feel.

"Making a kid is not a big deal," she would say. "Get two or three glasses of champagne in you, and bingo! Carrying it for nine months is a bit of a bother. But giving birth, what a horror! It seems absolutely abominable to me; it disgusts me and repels me. No. If someday I feel like having a kid, I'll adopt one. There are enough unhappy ones around who never asked to be born. That is, provided a lesbian succeeds in adopting one. You know the trouble they give us about that—what with our unnatural sex habits and our scandalous lives!"

They lived together for three years.

Dany under the spell, fascinated, deeply in love; Lise giving herself wholly to her, passionately, envelopingly. She turned the intelligent but uneducated hairdresser into a brilliant, amusing girl.

One day Lise left her—brutally and without softening the blow—for a Greek woman who looked like Irene Papas, whom she was in turn to walk out on two years later, leaving her just as heartbroken and desperate as she had Dany.

Lise, Dany, and I all belong to the race of conquerors. We often fall for some new set of eyes, some passing body, for through all of these faces that we caress we are in search of an ideal love, a perfect love, which we very well know can never be.

There are some perfect moments, some women who seem ideal—until the day when the chink in the armor appears, that tiny defect that suddenly smashes our idol for us. We can't put up with it. We turn away, and worrisomely return to our endless, doomed search.

But Dany and I try to arrange it so we leave our disappointed loves with as little hard feeling or hurt as possible. Lise on the other hand has always acted like a bulldozer; she is selfish and doesn't care how she shreds the heart that yesterday she loved. Yet her fascination is such and the impression she makes so deep that, once the pain has gone, her victims never bear her any grudge. They even remember it all with a kind of longing.

The years following Lise's departure were a time of superficial amorous adventures for Dany, quick, often-changing affairs that never led to anything.

Once, while on vacation, she met a nice married couple.

They saw each other again, back in Paris, and Dany didn't bother to tell them that she loved women. There just had been no special reason to.

During dinner, a short time later, the husband took out of his pocket a card advertising a women's cabaret, and waved it under Dany's nose, asking, "You acquainted with this?"

"Sure," she replied.

And they dropped the subject. His wife was a cute thing, but nothing more. Then—but let Dany tell it.

* * *

A couple of days later, the husband barged into my salon and without any introduction asked, "You like my wife?"

I could hardly say I didn't, even if she had been a pig. Which, I'm happy to say, she wasn't.

"You know, she likes you a lot. So, if you want . . ."

"Thanks," I answered. "I do like women, but my bed is a raft that only has room for two. Overload it and it sinks."

"No! No!" he assured me. "You've got me all wrong. I'd pay no attention to the two of you . . ."

He was insistent about it, and kept urging me. So, why not? I called up the young wife, and we made a dinner date. Then we stopped off somewhere for a drink, and went up to my place.

Catherine was charming, and seemed to love this new kind of love I was making to her. The night went by without our noticing. It was 6 A.M. by the time we came to.

"Heavens!" she exclaimed. "Michel'll be worried!"

So she phoned home and, from what I could hear, he was not at all happy.

"I didn't say for you to stay out all night," he was storming. "I just meant an hour or two."

OK, so Catharine was operating under remote control. What did I care? I wasn't in love with her.

"Come on home with me," she said. "It'll smooth things out."

And there we were at their place. Catherine went and made breakfast for all of us, awakened her two-year-old little girl, and we all had breakfast at the foot of the husband's bed. By this time he had gotten over his grouch and was the same nice guy he had been on vacation.

For a couple of weeks, everything was fine. She and I slept together in the bedroom, so she could hear the baby if she called, and Michel, the husband, slept on the living-room couch.

One evening the two of us got home from the movies a little later than usual, and found Michel ensconced in the middle of the bed.

"What are you doing there?" we asked.

"I'm sick of sleeping on the couch," says he.

Well, I wasn't going to be fazed by that. I had no intention of going back to my place. I was tired, and it was late, and it was cold outside. So, into bed all three, Catherine in the middle. He behaved like a real gentleman, didn't try any monkey business, and we slept like three little angels.

When morning came, however, the scene turned sour. I don't know whether he had been thinking it over during the night, and decided he didn't like being with two untouchable women. Because, I forgot to mention, but by now Catherine wasn't letting him get near her anymore either.

So in the morning Michel said to me, "I want you to break this off with Catherine. The little gag has gone on long enough."

"OK with me," I said.

And I was getting ready to leave, because I wasn't in love with Catherine, and being swept away with the wave of a hand like an unwanted fly didn't especially hurt me or make me sore. But Catherine took it differently.

"Well, if that's the way it is," she says, "I'm moving out."

And the two of us were off in a rented van, with the

kid's crib, and toys, and valises. Some fun! I started having the giggles on the stairs, as I was carrying the little girl: Look, I was thinking, here I am a daddy again!

Every Thursday, Michel would come to have dinner with us. Visitation rights, you might say . . .

And that went on for three months. Then, one evening, he looked intently at me and, in a very calm voice, articulating each word, very deliberately and thoughtfully, not at all in any sudden fit of anger, he turned to his wife, and said, "I warned you, Catherine. I'm going to kill Dany."

"If you do, I'll testify against you," she said.

"A woman is not allowed to testify against her husband."

And they were off in a big discussion about whether or not he could kill me without getting into too much trouble. I was in the middle, and turning from one to the other as the Ping-Pong ball bounced back and forth. That's not my favorite kind of situation.

He finally left, after slamming the door. And I convinced Catherine that the best thing for her to do was to go back home. She listened to me, but a month later she left him for good—to go live with another woman. I felt I could breathe a little easier. Michel would no longer have it in for me, and I hoped he'd stop using pictures of me for his pistol practice.

But I had misjudged him. Five years have gone by, and he still has it in for me, because he feels I'm the cause of the whole thing, and that I'm the one to blame for his wife having gotten into this life of debauchery. I keep hoping that, as time goes by, he'll forget about me!

* * *

Dany had definitely had it with men. The last "virile interlude" that she remembers was a bathetic episode that illustrates men's stupid illusions and their childish self-confidence.

She was still living with Catherine. Some friends were at their place for the evening. Drinks, talk, and among the guests there was a fellow who was supposed to be gay. When everyone else had left, he asked the girls if they could put him up for the night, because he had forgotten his car, or lost his keys, or some such excuse. They were quite willing to help him out of a bind. They made a bed up for him on the living-room couch, then went into the bathroom to take off their makeup and get ready for the night.

When they came out into their room, they found him there in the middle of their bed, looking smug as could be, propped up on the pillows, his arms extended in a suffer-little-children-to-come-unto-me pose.

"What the hell is this all about?" they demanded to know.

"I'm ready for the two of you."

"None of that, my friend. Out of there on the double, and get the hell out of here!"

They must have looked as though they meant it, in spite of the fact that they could hardly hold back their giggles when they saw him emerge from the bed, crestfallen but still ready for action: naked as a jaybird but his little cockadoodle cockadoodling.

He got into his socks and shoes, and shirt, and only then began to put on his shorts—leaving his dear little yoyo for everyone to see as long as possible, "just in case anybody might have second thoughts." For who, after all, can resist the enchanting vision of a man in his stocking feet, with his tumescent member waving in the wind?

To make a long story short, he went his way, tail between his legs, out into the cold dark city. But that reminds me of a letter I once got from a married woman, who was tired of what she had to put up with:

"I finally have understood what's wrong with my old man," she wrote. "He's always so proud to flash his 'thing' at anyone he can, always so sure that he'll never be turned down . . ."

* * *

What a need men have to try to mix into our female couples, even if only through indirect suggestion, as if we needed their ridiculous direction to run our enjoyments and our couplings!

I can remember one potbellied bald old man, a sea dog who looked like Yul Brynner, who had tried every trick in his bag to get Evelyne and me into bed with him, in vain. Finally, he suggested putting a lace cover, which he generously said he'd treat us to, over our bedside lamp.

When I looked surprised, he explained: "That way, there'll be flecks of shadow and light all over Evelyne's naked body, according to the pattern of the lace. And when you caress her, you'll be trying to rub away those dark spots, and you won't be able to . . ." His lips trembled gluttonously and his mouth was watering, at the mere idea of these idiots' delights that his genius had dreamt up.

What need have we for perverted subterfuges like that?

I don't need any man's advice to know how to make love to a woman.

Rather, the man ought to wonder about, yes, and worry about our loves, our caresses, our mysteries. Not merely the motions we go through, but the ritual we perform.

The value of each glance, each breath, each heart-to-heart contact, the invisible, the indiscernible, the undescribable . . .

And then there are the others, the ones who say to me, of an evening, "My wife [or my girl friend] would like to have a woman." The way she might like to have a steak or a baba au rhum. Not have a specific woman, because she has found her beautiful, or desirable, no, just to have a vagina, a tongue, a nameless hand . . . Fuckable flesh on the hoof? Not on your life! Anyway, it wasn't his wife or his girl friend who had the crude, naked desire, it was he himself, and he transposed it, interpreted it in his male head, with his male mentality.

Women rarely go out with the specific idea of screwing

in mind. They don't say (or think) to themselves, as they take that last look in the mirror before going out, "Tonight I've got to have a woman."

The phallus with the homing head is your appurtenance, gentlemen, not ours.

What we get is a desire to make love, and it's a diffuse desire that spreads through our entire body, that grabs us in the belly and the breasts, and parches our mouths and our lips. It's not merely the hardening of one specific member that just simply juts out to show its need.

No, we are not a machine that merely has to be turned on so it will work; we're not a teat that merely needs to be milked so it will start to spout and discharge.

Life went on for Dany. There was Greta. She was a German who worked at UNESCO, intelligent and cultured. They had a stable relationship, a love based on mutual respect and esteem, that lasted for two quiet, cloudless years.

At the end of that time, she was transferred to Vienna. Big heartbreak. And why? Because we cannot be married. We don't exist in the official, social, or professional lives of our mates. Our lives together are just mirages, our unions mere illusions. Greta left Paris. They did what they could to keep their feelings alive, but how can you live with your heart in the Prater and your body in Belleville, how can you nurture a love that can be expressed only two months a year? Life went on. Greta met an Austrian friend and Dany met Jane.

Jane! Not beautiful, no, fat, and masculine, her hair turning gray, and growing on her face, and she had a lousy disposition, but witty as could be. For Dany, intelligence has always meant much more than beauty.

In that, she and I are very different, and I've often been taken to task for the way I am attracted to, the way I idolize beauty in woman. I've even had girls throw it up to me, as if it were the final reproach: "You're just like men, the only girls you want are the beautiful ones."

So what? Just because I'm a lesbian, should I be condemned to love only ugly women? Should I be deprived of the right to sing, to celebrate the beauty of women because, being a woman lover, I have to accept all of them as they are? Should men alone be allowed to celebrate the beautiful ones, and to prefer them? Does the fact that I am as I am mark me down as being macho?

Just a minute. Not so fast. If that were the case, I wouldn't hesitate to line up with the men. Word of honor, even if it's thrown up to me for a thousand years, I'll go right on being attracted, enchanted, and bewitched only by a girl with lavender-blue eyes, a handsome body, a perfect face, bronze breasts, even if her heart turns out to be made of stone, even if under that soft hair of hers there be a shortness of ideas. Unpretty women exist, and I don't deny them the right to love and be loved, but I still have to be allowed not to want to take them all into my arms.

At any rate, there are the Danys, there will always be the Danys to whom what matters is intelligence and charm rather than beauty. Just as some girls will always be flowers looking for a queen bee who may be as old as forty (or even older, lucky for me!), and some will be fruits looking for the tart and delicious awkwardness of youth.

* * *

After that, there was Marie-Claire (Dany said). No, in between there was Jocelyne, a tiny little bit of a thing, not pretty but lively as a squirrel. She lived in Tours. I met her at some friends'. She only happened to be there by accident, because her husband had gone away for a skiing lesson, and someone was taking care of her three kids. Believe me, it's fated that way for me.

We would get to see each other afternoons, between trains. She adored women. You could tell it in every one of her movements, every one of her words. She liked her husband all right, he was a big good-natured bear, an innocent who was a million miles from imagining what kind of errands took his wife to Paris all the time. She had gotten married at twenty because "that was the best thing to do," because when you live in Tours and you're a doctor's daughter, it's unthinkable, impossible for you to come out as a lesbian. So she had married a nice, slightly bewildered gentleman, who seemed in need of protection, wanting a mother more than a wife.

When I met her she was thirty-seven, and the itch was getting pretty urgent inside her head. She was becoming obsessed—obsessed by the idea that she might have to die under the same roof with a man, in a bed that she would have shared all her life long with a man. It was crazy and heartbreaking to hear her talk about these things as she cried her eyes out after we made love.

And she was one to whom I couldn't say, "Well, leave your husband and come with your kids and live with me."

I didn't love her that much to begin with, and besides, three new kids for a girl to be the "unwed father" to are a bit much, don't you think?

Poor little Jocelyne! I don't know what became of her. Because that was when I met Marie-Claire and stopped seeing her. Maybe she got divorced, maybe she didn't. Because she had no way of making a living, and running off with three kids is a lot easier to dream about than to do. Can four people live in a single room? Can you go to a women-only hotel? Where do you farm the kids out? What do you live on? How do you make out?

I met Marie-Claire in the salon; she had come to have her hair done. She was beautiful, with gorgeous blue eyes, slightly misty as with all nearsighted people, and she was a girl who was a "brain," intelligent, brilliant even, but only when she feels among friends, because she's terribly shy.

At that time she'd been living with a boy for eight years. She didn't have any kids, and I never saw her guy, because she simply gave him his walking papers, came and stayed at my studio while he was moving out of her place, and then we moved into a larger apartment, not far from the salon.

I have no idea how she went about breaking off with him. She told me, "It's no concern of yours. Let me do the housecleaning in my life myself . . ."

The boy must have been a good guy, because he never came making a scene at my door, or pestering her by telephone, or any of those petty annoyances that often follow the breakup of any couple, straight or gay.

For eight years now, I've been living with Marie-Claire. On an automatically renewable lease . . .

Probably it's because I'm the first woman she's ever been with, and she looks on me as her guy and thinks it's perfectly normal for me sometimes to go out looking for a pickup, or have some kind of brief affair. These things are never any threat to our unity.

I don't think it's right for her to feel that way, incidentally. I'm not often unfaithful to her; it's only happened twice, and each time it was traumatic for me, though not for her. She doesn't seem to realize that I'm not a man, and that it's just not possible for me to make love without feeling anything meaningful about my partner.

* * *

Dany is neither a Casanova nor a Don Juan. What could those two have given to all the women they possessed?

Nothing. A bit of courtship, a little compliment, and bang! they knocked the poor girl over on the mattress. All that a woman meant to them was another prey bagged, only that and nothing more.

But for our part we leave a bit of our heart in every attachment we make. Even if we're not truly in love, we can't just *possess, hump, fuck, tear off a piece, screw,* or *ball.* When a man copulates, his heart may well be far away from the fun of it—assuming indeed that it is any fun!

But we make love. Which is to say, we create a unique moment that lasts an eternity.

The very term we use in French, *aventure*, to describe these amorous attachments of ours is full of mystery and unknown. An adventure—how can we know, when the courtship dance begins, whether our hearts will keep beating to this rhythm for a month or a year? The adventure of it is in finding oneself with heart overflowing, with one's arms linked around another's body!

And with one's soul aswoon. But when do we really know that for sure? After how many kisses, after how many nights?

* * *

What I prize above everything (Dany tells me) is my freedom. I detest feeling pent in. I can't breathe. That's the awful thing about women's jealous feeling of exclusivity. They want everything, demand everything. And when that happens, after a while, sooner or later, I've got to escape . . .

With Marie-Claire, it's wonderful, just because of that. She doesn't care if I go out alone, from time to time, with a gang of other girls, and she doesn't try to tag along. So we go out and paint the town, you might say . . . When I'm out like that, I may flirt with some pretty woman, which doesn't mean I'm going to go any further, but just that if I *want to*, I *can*. I feel completely free, free to bestow my heart where I will and make what motions I want.

Her family reacted amazingly. She immediately let them know she was leaving her guy to move in with a girl. They sulked for a week, and then asked to meet me.

They accepted the situation so naturally! It was merely a change of son-in-law to them, not a change of sex! My "father-in-law" brings in the bottle of after-dinner brandy and winks at me, as he pours a glass for himself and me, among us fellows, while my "mother-in-law" calls to my dog, "Come to Grandma."

The old man tells me about his odd jobs around the house, which are Greek to me, and she gives me cashmere sweaters for my birthday . . . We have a proper classical family situation, just because they accept me, refusing to see the "difference" between a man and me. It may be a little ridiculous, but it's awfully nice. And, in the final analysis, it makes life a lot easier and helps us be happy.

I know that I'm a reassuring type, I have a comforting and satisfying image for those who look at me objectively, because I have a comfortable situation, "an honorable trade," and in a word I'm dependable! That's undoubtedly why I always attract nonlesbian women and those who have kids.

Besides, when they don't have any, as in Marie-Claire's case, the minute they move in with me they start wanting to. She's done everything possible to try to adopt one. But finally she had to give it up, because there were so many obstacles. It turns out to be easier to have one the old-fashioned way.

Marie-Claire is a teacher. Naturally, she hasn't come out of the closet at the lycée where she teaches. If she were to let the people there know her life-style, they would never give it the kind of open-minded understanding they have when they study the strange ways and customs of Pygmies or Papuans.

So that's the way it is with us, Elula. As you can see, our life is at once very simple and very complicated. Full of women and passions. I have a salon that's doing well, a little country house down south in the Périgord, girl friends and pals that I get along with, a woman I love and who loves me. What more can one ask out of life?

When I started in in hairdressing, in the posh salon on the Faubourg Saint-Honoré, there were society ladies, rich bitches with snazzy perfume and mink coats, who tried rubbing up against me in the dressing rooms while they got into their robes. They were always trying to slip tongue kisses to me while their chauffeurs waited on the street below in their cars. They'd dangle money before my eyes, if I would only come to their houses for tea. But I always said No. I never made a secret of what I was—but I was never up for sale.

Of course, with my short haircut, people often say I look like a little boy. And men tell me that whatever I can do for a woman, they can do, too, with a little something extra besides. I think that little something extra is something just a little superfluous—something we can just as well do without, in any case.

Femininity, in the eyes of most men, corresponds to the length of your hair. A girl with long hair is "feminine," and they can't conceive of her really being a lesbian. And, of course, no real woman would ever turn them down. As one guy said to me one day, about Marie-Claire:

"Just leave your little friend alone with me for an hour and you'll see what happens! I'll bet you two cases of champagne I'll make out!"

Such smugness! They've changed old Caesar's line to "I see, I conquer, I come! No one can resist my virile prong!" If the poor bastards only knew how indifferent we could be to it!

Even the pitchmen on the Grands Boulevards don't sound that sure of themselves when they're reeling off their line. Every man is convinced he's a superduper ladykiller, he's Superman, Zorro, and Tarzan all rolled into one.

To me, they all will remain, forever, what they've always been: the Shadow and the Invisible Man.

JUDITH

"Her belly . . . It was delight such as I never would have believed could have existed . . . Burning, a burning oven, smooth, velvet-lined, laid with moist moss.

"Something like sinking into too warm a bath when you are frozen to the bone, or when you're lying nude on the beach getting the full force of the sun on your skin after it had been hidden for too long a time behind a screen of dark clouds.

"Perhaps like the amniotic fluid the baby bathes in inside its mother? Softness, sweetness, with a capital *S*.

"My fingers, numbed with the unbelievable feeling, moving slowly the better to become infused with it. And my lips, gone mad, my tongue doing its best to make her more streaming still, sweeter and softer yet.

"She moaned, emitted hushed, short, panting cries; then they got longer, bursting right up to my ears, their waves growing louder until they resounded inside my own belly, like magic waves; she finally shook violently, her belly beneath my palm grew hard; slowly, crawling up her magnificent body, slipping my face between her two firm breasts that were so round and beautiful, I reached her lips.

"They were just as cool as her belly had been hot. They were oasis, rain, and breeze.

"I transmitted to her tongue all the heat that my own had gathered from the hollow of her belly. A perfect circle had been completed. We now were but one body, but one breath, but one sign of happiness.

". . . She was the tenth woman with whom I was making love. Yet, it seemed to me that before her there had really been nothing; just some sensual games, a mere apprenticeship to prepare me for this universe I was barely discovering. The slow approach to her, my Eve, the first woman, for her alone. For her long warm neck into which I was now burrowing. For her still half-closed eyes that looked at me with so much love, oh, so much love! . . . For her body on which I was lying and which seemed to adhere to every square centimeter of my own, from our shoulders to the tips of our feet, along our thighs, our hard and soft bellies, her chest into which mine, so much tinier, so neatly fitted.

"I called her my Eve. I had whispered the name of the first woman as I in my turn was dying the little death under the ministration of her lips, inexpert as they were. But my desire was such, my arousal so violent, that I was bursting into a thousand stars before her fingers had even grazed me.

"As with all the others, I was in love with her, my nineteen-year-old Eve . . . her, as well as the other women who are my land of refuge.

"Is there anything more essential in my life than they? I love and detest them all at once, in a great insolent, violent whirly-go-round; the ebb and flow of my passions and affairs determine the very rhythm of my heart."

* * *

This is Judith speaking. Is she beautiful? She once was, to be sure; she is slim, wiry, dark, approaching fifty, but still equipped with many a trump, many an attraction.

* * *

I was married at eighteen (she goes on) to a fellow who was just as immature as I, an adorable mummer, a delightful sprite, who could be romantic when he was playing Musset, playful in Marivaux, energetic in Beaumarchais: He went on to have the theatrical success I was never to achieve. Let's call him Pierre. He was a good actor who adored his work. We shared a taste for the classics, the way we shared our meager student lunches. We dramatically rehearsed our sorrows and our worries in the gardens of Saint François-Xavier, next door to the school where we used to sit snuggled against each other on the uncomfortable benches, drinking in the professors' lectures on acting methods.

We got married as part protest, part dare. He was twenty and we thought we were in love; but when I said "I love you" to him, was I, Judith, really laying bare my heart, or was it just the aspiring actress in me learning how to play romantic roles?

Our marriage lasted one theatrical season. When the next season started—after we had spent two horrible vacation months up north at Douai with his family—I exploded like the good southern girl I am. Pierre had revealed himself that summer in his most unpleasant light. Always fastidious, he had become impossibly exacting, and I could well imagine what he might, and did, become—a real prissy type, a ham, a nitpicker—the very antithesis of everything I was and am.

We didn't split right away, though. We stayed together for a while in the two-rooms-and-kitchen his parents were paying for over near Rue Jouffroy.

I had successfully passed the entrance competition for the Dramatic Conservatory, but after three months I was given tactfully to understand that my attitude was not exactly what the faculty had in mind. I left without too much regret. I had rather thought I'd prefer acting in movies, anyway.

So I started making the rounds of the production offices on the Champs-Élysées. Especially their waiting rooms, with the world-weary secretaries who kissed you off with "Leave your composite if you want. Don't call us, we'll call you." And the occasional producer who said, "You got a good build. Go see my director about doing a pinup in one of my upcoming films." You go, and you find fifty other girls already there, all in bikinis, dying of the cold (while

I died of shame), the whole flock of us stamping our feet to overcome the gooseflesh, all so as to end up cast in the background behind Jean Marais in a dormitory scene. After which you can tell people, "See, that's me, just behind him there. You'll see, in a minute, I'll be smoothing my hair. Now . . . Don't blink . . . Did you see me?"

Pierre gave me food and lodging, and supported me. He was fine about it all. We had screwed a lot during the two years we were together, before and after we were married. He was ardent, thoughtful, tender, and had given me some sweet, diffuse satisfaction, but none of those homeric orgasms that make you roar like a lioness, no, rather just nice pleasant pleasures that left me purring like a pussycat in his arms.

When I decided not to be his wife any longer, he wondered why, in real surprise. "But—don't we get along well together?" he asked. "Aren't you happy with me anymore? Have I made you unhappy?"

"No, worse than that. You've sterilized me."

He didn't react violently to that, didn't hit me or hound me, didn't even yell or swear or cry. He just plain didn't understand; but he was so concentrated on his work—he was in his third year at the Conservatory at the time—that his suffering and dismay just became so many more emotions he could add to his bag of tricks. He threw himself wildly into it. Working like a demon, taking any walk-ons he could get in the evening, putting on shows with friends of his, burying himself in the profession he's done so well in.

And maybe I had something to do with that—by having been so youthfully ardent, so demanding, and then leaving him at the very dawn of his career.

Mine was mired down. My empty heart was on the lookout, my mind was in a whirl, and I no longer believed I had "the call." I didn't feel I could lay a production manager in the hope of getting a contract, and didn't feel like giving a casting director a quick blow job in his car just to get a bit part in a movie. So I went on letting Pierre see me through, and getting sick from my wounded pride.

Then, in a Latin American cabaret near the Montagne Sainte-Geneviève, for the first time I came into contact with women.

I had gone there to do a few poetry readings between guitar numbers. The two charming gay guys who ran the place had taken a liking to me right off.

Léo was mannish, but some hunk of a woman; she intrigued me, though I can't say I was attracted. She was a poet, a painter, a sculptor, and my meeting up with her was like a second birth, in both mind and flesh.

I didn't love her as well as she deserved. It was her appearance! She had terrific presence, but, unfortunately, was so masculine: She was stocky and looked as if hewn by a tomahawk. Clearly, she took after her Ecuadorian father.

Her short curly hair, jet black, straightened when it grew out and made her look even more fiercely like a Jivaro Indian. She looked absolutely indecent in a dress because she had the calves of a Greek hoplite, and with makeup she was as grotesque as a man in drag. Yet for all her extraordinary physical strength, she had a subtly feminine sensitivity and instinctiveness, which not every woman, even lesbian, always has.

She loved women, and could not love anyone but.

And she was able to get around me, to fascinate me, to reveal so much of the beauty of poetry and painting to me that I became like an ultra-sensitive photographic plate in her hands. The love she showered on me brought me out, and I wanted a chance in turn to try out this new power I had just acquired. My dazzled discovery of real sexual pleasure was something I now wanted to impart to others.

Léo was the kind who love to give but refuse to be taken. And I was still eager to get to know a woman's body, to explore the unknown body so like mine, to get to know the color of the cries you can provoke, to taste the fragrance of a skin, to touch the sex that was my own, vibrating now with so great an intensity.

Léo understood.

I had a devouring need for visible femininity. I was starving for the female form, for real women, femme women, not men-women or child-women, but sister women, as ardent as I myself, just as famished for passions, for wild loves, for bursting joys.

So she guided me gently toward extracurricular affairs. She closed her eyes to the fact that my cheeks were too flushed, my eyes too drawn when I came home. At night there were still her warm, tender arms to fall asleep in.

I was twenty. There was Nicole and Josiane, then Yvette and Marie-Alice.

I was out on love maneuvers, skirmishing over the terrain of sex, storming the weak points, taking prisoner the volunteers who joined in the sweet game of love. They were the same age as I, had the same hungers and thirsts, but also the same laughter and naïveté.

Léo found her consolation elsewhere, with a truly Rabelaisian truculence and verve, an expansive, robust joie de vivre that came through in her laugh, in her deep sensual voice, with its dignified, silent melancholy.

I think that we were a true couple, for we were united by unequaled devotion, total sincerity, a perfect identity of ideas and views on everything. "What really counts," she would say, "is all the rest. Sex, passionate lovemaking, can be found at any street corner, at every turn of the heart. But what there is between us, so light yet so solid, so invisible yet so real, these privileged bonds that we have woven between us, no one could ever break them. First they would have to recognize and see them, to know where to strike in order to separate us."

For seven years we lived together, ostracized from "polite society," not by men (who had the best of comradely relations with her, without ulterior motives, for good and proper reasons) but by women: Certain female members of the bourgeoisie, both lower and upper, suddenly in a fit of jealousy and possessiveness turned out to be veritable Furies.

But Léo was solid as a rock. She had been a lumberjill in the Chevreuse Valley during the Nazi occupation, and later a house painter. She was now her own boss in a house-painting and decorating business that did very well with the female clientele.

We hung out around Saint-Germain-des-Prés, with its cafés and night spots, and in the dance halls on the Montagne Sainte-Geneviève, and places like that.

One day in early March, I was on vacation in my house on a hill down south (they claimed that it had once been a hunting stop for the Gascon king of France and Navarre, and today as then you could only get up there on foot or on muleback), with a tender lovemate.

That very day, Léo died tragically in an auto accident near Aubagne.

The next day I had a letter from her, telling me she was on her way back. I had no idea at the time that it came from beyond the grave . . .

I couldn't believe the news (which was kept from me for more than a week). For a presence like hers to be so brutally torn away! Then I had to face up to it. I tore off my clothes (literally), and ran off naked into the mountains, on a freezing early morning in March, and lay down on the ground, on the cold stones, as if to dig down into the earth. She had loved me with the love of a troubadour-knight as it is described to us in courtly romances.

I was bursting out of my body, which was too narrow to hold so huge a sorrow. I wanted to gouge out my eyes no longer to see what she could not see: the spring that was now aborning, nature that she so dearly loved . . .

Lying flat on my back in bed, my head thrown back,

motionless, weeping and moaning, I felt two tears drop on my lips, like two drops of dew. It was Monique, my spring flower, giving me a good-bye kiss. She understood, and was leaving, so I could remain with my dead, divining that for a long time to come I would be able to belong only to the past.

Haggard, speechless, somnambulistic, like an empty chrysalis, devoid of substance, for months all I heard was a voice inside me—my own voice—endlessly repeating, "Love is dead, love is dead."

Out of some vital need for expression, I began to write, to work by myself, even though my gregarious instinct has always carried me toward circuses, street entertainers, theaters.

Washed up on the shore of my bed like an empty shell, I was awaiting the spark that always seems to me so slow in appearing. What wanderlust is it then that makes me become poor Lazarus at the banquet, a beggarwoman inside my own kingdom, a blind person in the brightest sunlight? Yet a shadow, a faithful, watchful shadow, follows me in the rays of a dark sun that has the bright-red ardor of passion, and I am reborn once again from my ashes . . .

Slightly out of breath, I tear along, limpingly, behind a light-footed muse. And then before each blank page, I have to learn again how to write, as one discovers love all over again with each new passion.

To sing of woman—but how would I be able to? Time covers my most sumptuous memories with even more sumptuous alluvial deposits that make a halo around the truth, and by that very fact alter it.

Yet, one had to survive. Without Léo, I couldn't carry on our decorating trade. What do you do when all you know how to do is all and nothing? When you've been raised on Verlaine and Lorca, sometimes sketching some felicitous ensembles for idle bourgeois housewives, when you've lived under the comfort of a guardian genius?

I went into an insurance company as an agent, a catch-all job, either the last round or the first rung in a career, that comprises the worst and the best, and you have to fight tooth and nail to hang on, for so many are called. I was one of the chosen. For three years I served well and loyally. With a desert in my heart and my gut. Yet it was in this job that I met Tania.

I was thirty, Tania was thirty-five. She was the one who made the first light passes, and the first real advances. I was amazed. She was so feminine, seemed to be the very model of a proper little wife. I had imagined her to be married, with a clutch of well-kept babies, simmering daubes and ragouts for a puttering husband—and discovered to my amazement that she loved ladies, and ladies only, ever since the husband, whom she had married ten years earlier, ran off with one of the lesbian friends she had introduced to him.

What immediately attracted me to Tania was her infinite sweetness. She was loving-kindness incarnate. Tania was good, in the way one can say that bread is good.

She got me out of my funk. I fell in love with her. We had met at the office, during an office party of the kind that always take place in big businesses, and since then her Ext. 32-28 had become familiar to me.

I phoned her several times a day, or else went over to her department, without any special reason, thinking ahead of some fancy excuse, some pretext, some need to be there. It was the thrill of a beginning love, the meeting of eyes and hands, the half-words half-spoken.

I lived with her for two years. Ought I to admit it? I tired of her quickly. She was not able to be both lover and sister, that symbiosis between Léo and my other affairs. What I was in search of was the ideal woman, and she was just simply a woman. She gave me everything that she had to give. Her warm and ardent body, her sweetness, her tenderness, her love. But I was cold—I could only become lukewarm. I had thought I was in love with her, but she had only been a mad hope. A disappointed hope.

What else was there? Well, I stayed on out of empathy, because life together was nice and quiet. We lived in a little cottage her parents had left her at Bagneux, outside Paris, with two Siamese cats, Bing and Bang, who had curly tails, broken voices, and cream-colored fur, among rosebushes that she clipped expertly, and nice neighbors whose two little boys we baby-sat when they went out with other couples.

I was sinking in deeper and deeper. I was suffocating. In the everyday and the expected, the planned and the scheduled, down into it up to my waist, to my chest, to my neck.

Tania never understood why I slept with Jacques.

Frankly, did I ever understand it either?

Was it that I was afraid of this monotonous life with a woman, this pseudo-monogamous marriage, and that I thought at that moment that if I were to be part of a couple it would be better with a man? Was I trying to escape from life with Tania or just from Tania herself?

Jacques came into my life by chance, at a painting show at the Galerie Charpentier, to which I had gone alone. He was a well-spoken, courteous man, a professor of literature who taught in Morocco, and he interested and amused me. I had forgotten what fun it was to laugh. We saw each other off and on for a month, once or twice a week, at museums, or in tea shoppes, crazy timeless kinds of places in which I was setting foot for the first time in my life, totally bemused and amused at the ageless ladies who indulged their idle gluttony there.

He was most charming, forty years old, slightly thin at the temples but with a face blue with a heavy beard that he had to shave twice a day. He was tall and slim, and smelled of lavender and tobacco—not unlike Léo . . .

Was it the memory of that, that superficial sentimentality, that kept me from pushing him away when finally, one afternoon, he kissed me good-bye? We were in my car, and I was letting him kiss me right there on the street, with passersby all around us, savoring the new pleasure of being able to allow myself to be kissed without embarrassment or care because I was with a man—savoring the pleasure of the unforbidden fruit—a new pleasure for a lesbian who was used to having to hide her loves in dark corners.

The next day we made love. I renewed contact with the male member without feeling either disgust or pleasure. Jacques made love to me as most men do. That is to say, after a fleeting exploration by mouth and by hand, completely without effect because it was so inexpert, he quickly got around to the inevitable in-and-out, push-and-pull which is supposed to develop into a galloping twosome but in which the male rides off by himself on a single-minded dash to climax—and the only thing it has going for it is that it ends so blessedly quickly.

I didn't even feel that general well-being I had experienced with Pierre. But it wasn't orgasm that I was after.

What I wanted was a different life, a life like all the rest of the people in the great majority lived.

I had given in easily, because Jacques seemed very much in love with me. He was leaving for Morocco again the next month and urged me to go with him. I was holding out for a full-fledged proposal. I got it right after our first love bout. I asked for a week to think it over, but my mind was already made up.

I was going to leave sweet little Tania, give her back her freedom, and resume mine—only to give it up again immediately.

That very evening I let Tania know I had screwed a man. She was bug-eyed, sure I was kidding her. She kept repeating, "Not you, not you. I can't believe it. You love women too much."

"I want to live a *normal* existence, Tania," I told her. "It has nothing to do with my love for women."

"But if you just want to lay a fellow from time to time, there's no reason we can't go on living together. I won't hold it against you."

It was a dialogue of the deaf. She was willing to let me have my little affairs with men, like a husband who doesn't forbid his wife to have girl friends. Whereas the facts were just the opposite: I didn't want girl friends anymore; I wanted a husband.

She wept. She swore at me. She called me a tramp and a whore. She phoned the few lesbians we went around with, to say, "Judith is fucking guys."

I became the guilty one, accused of every kind of vice. I couldn't have cared less. I packed my things, leaving to Tania all the furniture and other things we had jointly bought. All I took were my personal effects. I wanted to start afresh in a fresh skin.

Jacques didn't know anything about my past life. Or rather, I had told him about Pierre, but nothing about the women that there had been in my life. They were no concern of his, and they didn't matter since I had determined I would be a good wife. Buried deep in my memory, my past loves were no one's business but my own. All I had told him was that I had been sharing a cottage with a woman friend . . .

We got married in Fez, where he taught.

Three years.

I held out for three years.

For three years Jacques held me in his arms, every evening, every night. He was an adorable, amusing mate, without complications or problems. He rarely mentioned his first wife, who had died five years before. From her pictures, she seemed a rather colorless woman, who had been a fellow student of his at the university. He had married her at twenty, the same as me and Pierre . . .

Three years.

Three years of love on his part, friendship on mine. Three years of joyless nights, during which I pretended an enjoyment I was not experiencing. Not even those near-orgasms I had had with Pierre. A man's body, a man's cock, his hand, his mouth could not take the place of a woman. All women, any woman.

Was I honest with myself? Oh, yes, I swear I was, I swear it by the eternal feminine.

And if little by little, like a cancer, the image of women wormed its way into my mind, my brain, my dreams, my fantasies, my imagination, becoming ever more lifelike, more real, more appealing, more tenacious, it was not for want of trying desperately to hang onto Jacques's shoulders, for want of outdoing myself in making love to him, caressing him, licking his body, sucking his cock, in the hope of achieving my pleasure by heightening his.

All in vain. The more time went by, the more the image of woman reared itself within me, monopolized me, sweeping everything away in its path, obsessive, ever-present.

For no specific reason, one day Jacques's caresses became unbearable to me. The repulsion and disgust that had slowly been settling in broke out like a thunderclap; I turned hostile, sullen, distant, even odious.

I could no longer stand this man who thought that I was his, and a good wife, who hoped I would decide to want a baby, and purred with satisfaction in his happy home which was a snare and a delusion.

"I'm a lesbian, I can't stand it anymore!" my whole body was shouting. "Let me return to women. Let me have my women again. Jacques, sweet husband, poor Jacques, I have been deceiving you from the very first day. I thought I could overcome my own deeper nature. I'm the one who's at fault. But now let me leave. Don't touch me again, or I'll scream. My skin is burning up, my belly is crying out with emptiness, my lips are as parched as the earth of a dried wadi. A woman's skin, a woman's kiss, a woman's flower, for the love of heaven!"

But he didn't catch on.

I left like a thief in the night. What else could I do? Try to explain to him? If he had understood, might he have suggested, as Tania had, that he would close his eyes to my extracurricular activities?

Out of the question! I'm not one for compromises. Perhaps he would have wanted to help me by having me go into analysis. But I wasn't sick. I was just a lesbian!

I left him a long letter, telling him all about it. I asked him not to try to get me back. The whole thing was a pitifully melodramatic situation. I went to Casablanca, to stay with friends. They lent me some money for a ticket. I got back to Paris, alone, with two suitcases. Three years after my triumphal departure, here I was back again at the same point: starting fresh, and traveling light . . .

I got a job right away, through *France-Soir* my first day back. As a pollster for a private, with a company car. A perfect setup!

For four years I knocked around all over France, crisscrossing it from top to bottom, from left to right. I just had a tiny furnished room in Paris, as a haven between my many hotel rooms. I was living it up but in an intellectual and emotional desert. I was getting to put some money aside, by doing without whatever I could, paying a premium price for my newfound freedom.

I remained alone a long time. In spite of everything, I had been traumatized by my marriage to Jacques; and, quite the opposite of what might have been expected, when I first got off the plane I hadn't thrown myself at the first woman I saw. I still ached too much from my disastrous experience, was too disoriented by it all. I had to get through my convalescence in order to want to live again and to love. It was only much later that I finally met Eve.

She was studying law and was bored with it. We kept looking at each other all evening. I asked whether I could see her home. In the car, we went at it right away, without beating around the bush, without introductory small talk, almost brutally. She was nineteen, and had a she-wolf's teeth, and blond bangs that came down over her eyes. We went back in for a last cup of coffee—amazed by what we had just done. Our cheeks were aflame—with embarrassment? Or was it that we were still slightly out of breath from our hasty climax sitting there in the car, fearful of possibly being caught in the dark street along the River Saône?

We laughed.

"I want to see you again."

"Me, too."

My hand went to hers, and grazed it. Her aroma must have lingered on my fingertips, as mine lingered on hers.

"I'll be in Évian for the weekend."

"I'll meet you there."

I was febrile, impatient, excited.

That week seemed like an eternity to me. I went to my appointments with my mind on other things, returned at night to my various hotel rooms, and scribbled beside my notes sketches of her face, her body that I hardly knew yet, that I had had so fleetingly.

On Sunday morning, I woke up at six. She was arriving at noon. The day before, I had been out casing the lakeshore areas. I wanted a beautiful, romantic room, with a view on the lake, obviously. I found one. It cost me three days' pay. It could have wiped out a month's salary, for all I cared.

What I wanted was huge, wide beds in which I could

listen to her moan, make her cry out again and again without worrying about thin walls. What I wanted was beauty.

I moved in slowly. I killed hours rearranging a vase, an ashtray, setting the radio just right at the head of the bed, trying different lightings. It was as if she were already there with me.

At eleven, I was at the station.

What if she were to stand me up?

But she came out through the little gate, carrying her valise. Stiff hellos, barely touching kisses, reticent hands. And banal exchanges: "We're sure lucky to have this kind of weather." The trip back. My hand on her knee. Hotel, elevator, bellboy showing us in, room, tip, door closed.

Eve was standing against the light, looking at the lake. We hugged each other for a long moment, arms tight, silent, listening to each other breathe, feeling our hearts beat a little faster, sensing the slight trembling of our legs, the tremor in our thighs.

Slowly, my mouth started to move. My lips grazed her cheek, her neck, her hair, my hands came up to her face, holding it, framing it. Eve's eyes were green—as I imagined the algae at the bottom of the lake.

The sun was shining just a bit too warmly for June. Our lips finally met, our tongues discovered each other, first motionless, then slowly, sweetly, caressing each other, learning to know each other, turning one around the other, mixing salivas, merging new tastes.

I was determined to make this approach last a good long time. I was determined to erase the memory of our first meeting, that short animal encounter. I wanted *this* to be our first time together.

In fact, this was the first time I really desired Eve, and therefore everything remained to be discovered.

We slowly undressed each other, still standing, as if we

were performing a dance that had no end. I got down on my knees to take off her jeans. She was wearing a little girl's white underpanties. Her thighs had a golden down that was soft against my cheek.

I was fifteen years older than Eve, fifteen women more to my credit, and yet I was atremble with bashfulness just as much as she.

We were wearing next to nothing. Outside, it had started to rain. A violent shower was drumming on the lake. Slightly drunk with each other, we staggered from wall to wall, over to the bed. And slowly sat down.

She had beautiful breasts. I took them in my hands, which became wavering cups, from which I drank them, inhaled them, eager but restrained, as their tips hardened beneath my lips; the aroma of her arms surrounded me, she bent toward me. Her hair smelled like new-cut grass.

A local folk group had started to play. We could hear the shouts of dancers, the festivities going on out there.

I was lying against her, our legs intertwined caressingly. Our kiss was endless. Can one come in a kiss? I didn't know it.

We moaned at the same time. Eve, Eve, I love you, but I'm not going to say it.

Because ours is an impossible love, and tomorrow we'll be saying good-bye forever.

Because you'll go back to studying law in Lyons, and I'll go back to my wandering around the country.

Because there can be nothing in common between us but this unique moment, this one solitary night.

Yet, Eve, how I love you, how I'll always love Évian, and its lake, and the ridiculous yodeling outside that made us laugh hysterically after our first moans.

You can't make love to the sound of cornets! I hopped out of bed and went to close the window.

And then we made love, and I called her Eve because

she was all women, and all the others could never again be anything but a more or less perfect image of the love we had known.

We never left the room. We nibbled at the tray we had ordered, between kisses, between caresses. *We couldn't spare the time.* In one short night, we had to live the love of an entire lifetime, experience all, discover all, try all, exhaust everything.

I close my eyes and can still see her hand lying on her cunt, as upon the strings of a guitar. Her fingers softly, almost tenderly twitch, playing the deepest chords, a muted, slow lament. Her thin, elegant, mobile knuckles. Her almond-shaped nails, polished, gleaming, pearls in a setting of gilded velvet, their orients changing, gleaming in the half-light. I was fascinated.

"Caress yourself some more," I whispered in her ear, as she began moaning louder and louder. Her moans stretched out longer and longer, and soon were to become that monotone keening which would then give way to panting, as if she were mustering all of her strength in order to reach deep within herself to bring out that bursting cry, starting dully but swelling and swelling until at last it filled the room, went beyond the alcove, ran out into the hallway, the other rooms, sweeping away all familiar noises, covering everything, unique, the cry of love.

Out of some stupid modesty, I smothered that explosion of joy, I stuffed my hand into her mouth, urging her, "Bite, bite!" aching for her teeth to sink into my flesh, as if delving into my gut.

I never saw her again. Before I took her back to the station, we exchanged one last long kiss, as long as a whole lifetime.

I went back on the road, disabused and happy, sad and full of an unequaled happiness. I was like a pilgrim who had seen the light. I knew that God existed and that She had the face of a woman.

I knew that henceforth I was totally and truly *anandrous*;* meaning "free of men." I knew that from now on their paths and mine would never cross again. We were engaged on parallel pursuits. We could establish courteous relationships as good neighbors and fellow travelers, but one doesn't necessarily invite the neighbors, however charming they may be, to come in and share one's life.

There's an old Chinese proverb that says, "One teapot may fill ten cups; but ten teapots will be useless if there is only one cup to fill."

One man would be enough to repopulate the entire earth with the thousands of spermatozoa swimming around in every drop of his semen. Just one man . . .

All those useless, useless penises! Just sort of ornamental appendages. You can well understand the reason for all that cock-of-the-walking around: a normal compensation reaction!

They feverishly decree that they are the masters, and from time immemorial have acted as if they actually were.

Whereas in fact they're terrified deep in their guts. Terrified of their uselessness, the fragility of their unjustified power, terrified of the fact that without woman, without just one woman, a single one, the last man would die alone, desperately grabbing at his sterile belly, his useless rod.

They have gotten even by enslaving woman. Turning her into just a belly, precisely, a matrix, a mold. For fear that women might conceive the idea of a world without men, which is so easy to envision, they have kept women from thinking, from using their brains. They have held

---

* What a felicitous word that is! Too bad it hasn't come into the general vocabulary in place of all those harsh-sounding epithets that are applied to us.

them down in ignorance, in uneducation, from the darkest of early times.

So that they might not realize that they are the mistresses of the world and its fate, that they are the blood of the earth, whereas the men are nothing but the humble spark needed for the first fission of the egg.

I adopted a little girl, a little Vietnamese, whose refugee parents turned her over to me seven years ago. For, it goes without saying, no lesbian can legally adopt a child. Everybody knows our life-style is too immoral for us to have the custody of a child. Better to leave them as public wards than let them be around during our nights of rutting homosexuality and our depraved orgies! But enough of those bitter jokes: Little Mai lives with me and calls me Maman. She was only two when her parents let me take her. I know they have left for Gabon, where they are trying to rebuild their lives, and I don't imagine that for the moment they have any urge to take back their little Mai, who is their fifth child. Not so long ago, in Vietnam, people used to sell their offspring, and I confess that I'm counting on that attitude to let me keep Mai with me as long as possible, until she has blossomed into a fine young girl, and—who knows? with a little luck—perhaps a ravishing lesbian.

SYLVIE

Sylvie is thirty-seven, but she doesn't look it. What woman, nowadays, if she pays attention to her body, her weight, her complexion, and knows how to dress to suit her build, really ever looks her age?

I know some old women of twenty, mean-faced, sulky-mouthed, harsh-eyed, greasy-haired, while some of my "girl friends," now pushing fifty, keep lustily alive and slim, lightly made-up, having merely discarded the T-shirts that emphasized a slightly fallen set of breastworks.

At thirty-seven, Sylvie looks ten years younger. She isn't beautiful, but she's piquante. Her face is slightly pointed, her hair cut very short. Medium-sized, with firm little breasts that she gleefully allows to peep through the décolletage of the somewhat overlong men's shirts she always wears unbuttoned.

As far as her love life was concerned, I didn't really know anything. She wasn't readily confiding and always covered what she said with a somewhat mocking, blasé smile.

That summer, Joëlle and I, and Sylvie and her friend Danièle, had been invited to stay at the place Vanina, the gynecologist, and her girl friend had at Ronce-les-Bains, near Royan.

It was a big house, full of wind and iodine smells. At high tide, the sea washed up to the front doorsteps.

While Joëlle and Danièle, who were very athletic, went hiking down as far as the Côte Sauvage until they were nothing but tiny dots down there among the wrecked barks that lay on their sides like abandoned toys, Sylvie and I would lie in the sun—and talk.

That is, *she* talked, rather. A lot. To my surprise. She allowed me to lift some veils, to peek at some dark corners she hadn't wanted to remember. As the hours went by, and we felt a sense of complicity, impalpable but nonetheless real, Sylvie started to talk about herself, and all I had to do was listen to this woman whose life was unknown and incomprehensible to me, since it was so utterly different from my own.

Yet, the conclusion was there, to be seen by all. By very different trajectories, hers determined by men, mine by women, we had now come together in the same love we shared: that of woman and femininity.

* * *

"I've known a lot of men," she told me. "Oh, yes, lots of them. How many? I wouldn't be able to begin to count. No, not even if I tried hard. And besides, what does it matter? I don't remember any of them, they meant so little.

"The last one was in Paris, nine years ago, just after I arrived in France. What was his name? I don't think it makes much difference. Maybe it was Gérard. No, Gérard was a forester back in Abidjan, on the Ivory Coast. But then, maybe it was Gérard, at that.

"I was twelve when I had intercourse for the very first time. You must understand that at twelve I looked fifteen or sixteen. My blond hair came all the way down to my waist, and I had a well-developed figure. My father ran the officers' mess there. And in the swimming pool I was always on display, diving, swimming, shimmering like a carp.

"The fellow was a bartender at the pool. A real athlete, kind of a lifeguard type. He was very nice to me, as everyone was, and I guess I must say that, if things went as far as they did, it was partly my fault. I would hang around wherever he was, rubbing up against him like some kind of feline. And at first all he did was kiss me back in the stock room, my first kisses on the mouth. I thought it was too wonderful for words. Especially because, without her knowing it, I was getting a leg up on my big sister, who was three years older than me. I was very proud of myself, even if nobody else knew about it. I felt that I had become a young lady, not a kid anymore.

"Little by little, our games took a less innocent turn. He began to play with me, and taught me how to play with him.

"The first time he put my hand on his pecker, which was still soft, the warm feel of it wasn't the least bit displeasing. But then, when it started to get hard, I was kind of scared. You know, a man's penis isn't really very pretty."

"I'm well aware."

"Oh, yes! That's right, you've been married! Well, I can tell you, they haven't changed since your time, they're still just as ugly. And then he started to teach me . . . And that was when I really got turned off. The whole push-and-pull business, the massaging, seemed shocking to me. It's very unaesthetic. I didn't want to go on. But he held my hand enclosed in his, and I could feel the skin beneath it sliding back and forth . . . Yuch! . . . Incidentally, you know it's true that lovemaking with women is innate in a woman. I didn't have anything to learn the first time that I slept with a woman. I knew right away just what I ought to do, like on my own body, whereas a man has to *teach* us how to do him."

"And yet, see how paradoxical it is: A man's willing to teach us how to make love to him, but he rarely allows a woman to show him how he ought to caress her."

"Yes, as if they knew it all. And then they're surprised when their wives leave them for a woman!"

"But did it hurt the first time you let your handsome bar boy go all the way with you?"

"No. I don't really remember it. It didn't hurt, but it wasn't very good for me either. It didn't do any more for me than his earlier petting, which I had liked, had done.

"I only had an orgasm once. One day when I didn't want to let him get inside me. I was holding my thighs tightly pressed together, and as his hand rubbed against my clitoris it made me come.

"The other times, his hand would wander around kind of aimlessly; and yet, I think I was really and truly in love with him . . .

"That went on for two or three months, and then I came to France for the summer vacation, and when I got back to Tananarive, he wasn't there anymore. But I got over it very quickly. At twelve, you know, those little games don't seem all that important! I was just as happy, if not happier, to be playing tennis, or to be going out into the backcountry with my father. After that interlude, two or three years went by without anything else of the sort occurring. I think I was sixteen before I got screwed by a boy again. He was eighteen, on his summer holiday down south, and I guess I had a crush on him. He used to swipe his father's car, a convertible, and I was proud as a peahen to be seen riding around in it. But, as far as the physical part goes, I don't remember anything."

"I wonder how come, since you had been so well 'awakened,' you never thought of taking a little side trip on the feminine side."

"Probably just because the opportunity never presented itself. But it was just as well that way, because when it did finally happen, I was able fully to appreciate it. It was no longer kids' play.

"I passed my examinations and went to the University of Montpellier, to try for a law degree, after mooning around a year in psychology. None of the subjects was really my cup of tea. I wanted to go traveling, to get out of France, where I felt cooped up, since I had always lived in wide-open spaces in big houses surrounded by expansive verandahs that opened onto exuberant gardens.

"So I left for Abidjan, thanks to some connections of my

father's. I stayed there for six years. My boss was a terrific guy, a kind of force of nature. He weighed over two hundred and sixty pounds and was like a rhino that swept everything before him as he went. Sometimes we'd be off in the hinterland for a week at a time, buying cordwood, sleeping in the villages, up and away at dawn, slithering through the *poto-poto*, that mud that terrifies newcomers but through which I loved tó drive the Jeep and succeed in pulling out without having to be towed.

"He was a wonderful guy. Naturally, we screwed a few times, on a casual basis. It wasn't an obligation imposed on me, or a chore, no, it was just that the natural culmination of our friendship, our general mutual understanding, was for us to have sex together.

"Later on, he became my accomplice, my confidant. With his forty years and his upward of two hundred and sixty pounds, he wasn't quite cut out anymore for the mattress calisthenics of a young gymnast, and he was never jealous of the young lads who passed through between my sheets."

"And still no suggestion of a woman on the horizon?"

"Not the least. Of course, I had had crushes on my schoolmistresses, like everyone else, but nothing beyond that. And then, after Peter, Paul, Vincent, François, and all the others, the great lay that I had become met Nadine.

"Why her? God alone knows. She wasn't any more beautiful than other women I'd met in the course of my life. And yet, it was love at first sight.

"She came on the scene at Abidjan with two little daughters, a widow of six months' standing, to teach math. And moved into the apartment right next to our office. The minute I saw her, I was hooked. Such elegance, such grace, such bearing! She was the lightning bolt that strikes an entire landscape, burning everything away and leaving nothing from the past. I drowned in her much-too-blue eyes. I was done for . . .

"She was still very much affected by her widowhood, and I, in my selfishness, was the happiest woman in the world. It was as if, at one stroke, the bark of the tree had been slashed away, and now my heart, which had never truly beaten before, was at last revealed for what it was.

"I discovered everything with Nadine: beauty, the poetry of sound and words. I was now living only through her and for her. Nothing was too good for her little girls. My passion was plain to see, and Nadine had undoubtedly taken note of it, but she never let on. I never even thought of making love with her."

"Why not?"

"Because I wasn't a lesbian—or, at least, I didn't think I was, just because I loved a woman. One day, she said to me, 'If it hadn't been for you, I would have died of sorrow.' If you only knew how happy that made me. No, truly, I didn't *feel* I was a lesbian, or else I would never have egged her on so to get married again, to remake her life. It never occurred to me that she might remake it with me. I was a woman, after all. And woman, I stupidly believed, was conceived to go toward man like the female socket is fashioned to receive the male plug, to allow the electricity to flow."

"Well, that's correct, if you take it for granted that children are the electricity, the be-all and end-all of the meeting of plug and socket. But in broad daylight, for instance, there's nothing to keep the male or female parts from cavorting separately along the baseboards or walls."

"Except that that doesn't seem self-evident when nothing in your earlier life has given you any reason to suspect it. I remained 'just like everyone else' by accident, out of ignorance, only because I had never had a chance to discover my real sun.

"Nadine took my advice. She married a schoolteacher like herself, who was divorced and had one child. I think she's had a happy life. We kept writing to each other for a long time, but then, time went by, life went its way . . ."

"But didn't it hurt you, weren't you a little jealous at least, when she got married again?"

"No, because I simply *couldn't* conceive of any other outcome. You can't be jealous of the impossible. A goldfish can't be jealous of a bird, or a flower of a butterfly. They belong to different species. Women, for me, at that time were—how should I put it?—not exactly competitors, no, I never felt petty feelings of rivalry toward women, but rather saw them as colleagues, as pals, with probably the feeling about them that a soldier has for the other guys in his barracks. No more than that. Then, suddenly, there was this woman that I loved or by whom at least I was *enthralled*. But at that time I wasn't about to question all the world's values just because of that. I was too young; I was twenty-five . . .

"It was the next year that I slept with a woman for the first time. She was the one who came on to me, who made the advances. She was thirty-five and a newspaperwoman. She had come to spend three months in Abidjan to start a magazine, one of those big things on coated paper, with great layout and fine finish, financed by a big multinational corporation and never seen or read by anybody except in a doctor's or dentist's waiting room.

"She was a lifetime lesbian. I don't think she'd ever had any relations with a man, and was none the worse off for it. She herself was very butch, with short hair, and given to hitting the bottle a little too much, but of superior intelligence.

"She immediately recognized me for what I was. According to her my homoerotic preferences were as plain as the nose on my face. Because she saw a kind of casualness in my relations with people, something about me that was too direct, too outspoken, ever to belong to a straight chick. She had me wrapped up and tied in a bundle in no time, and when I came to I was in her bed."

"Weren't you shocked? Especially since you had never dared make a pass at Nadine, even though you loved her?"

"No, not really . . . You know, I've never been a prude, and nothing had ever scared me about the sex play with boys. So nothing she did to me could shock me. Rather, it turned me on, once my first surprise was over. And, as I was telling you before, I didn't have to learn any of the movements, there was nothing she had to teach me. It all came naturally, because she was a woman, like me, and her body was familiar to me, her reactions and desires easy to predict. We spoke the same language. We were from the same place."

"What was it that struck you the most when you washed up on these shores that were new to you?"

"The odor, I think . . . Yes, that was it. The odor of woman, so different from that of man.

"You know, the blacks in Africa say that whites have the smell of corpses, a bland, sweetish smell. And the musky black finds it hard to breathe in our aroma, just as we may find his smell strong. Well, in the same way, the odor of a woman's armpit is less upsetting to my sense of smell than that of a man's."

"I couldn't agree with you more. When I have to go into the men's lavatory, the odor of their urine constricts my throat, much worse than that of cat piss, which is strong enough. That is why I can understand very well how men's stomachs can sometimes be turned by a woman's vaginal smell, wishing that it tasted like Lux or smelled like Palmolive, whereas to me it is something that dilates my nostrils, as I burrow into the dusky bushes and encounter the excitement of the evening or the warmth of a day. Americans rinse their oysters off before downing them. Gourmets, to the rescue! Rinsing, asepticizing a shellfish? Why not perfume it with lavender or fern?

"If a woman's sex, that sacred shellfish, is to be scoured, and doused with patchouli oil, why not also pluck out all its hairs, and mask it off so as to reveal only the clitoris and the vulva?

"A woman's sex, that food, that drink with its aromas heavy or light, powerful or barely discernible, the sex which is the personality of each woman—how can anyone want to make it uniform, anonymous, stereotyped, to geld it by feminine hygiene deodorants, that latest invention of misogynists?"

"You're right. That is something else dreamed up by men who hate women. Another proof of their instinctive revulsion from our sex organs, of the dizzying fear that seizes them in front of the unknown abyss from which they came, but which they are now afraid to go back into."

"Yes, the *vagina dentata*, that biting vagina or 'snapping pussy' that the ancients and the moderns have talked about, the fear of castration, of letting their penises venture into an unknown organ that will always remain terrifying because it is mysterious.

"But not for us women, who know what the insides of our own guts are like, who are aware of the palpitations of our uteri, the contractions of our cervixes, the sensations you feel when the walls of our passages are touched . . . No, a woman's belly is nothing fearsome to us, and we know just what is being felt by the woman we hold in our arms, the woman we go down on, the woman we love.

"But all of that is getting us far afield from the odors you were telling me about, Sylvie. Excuse me for having gotten quite so lyrical—shall we say?—over something that is actually so prosaic."

"Not prosaic at all. But essential, like everything else that concerns women and the understanding of our inversion. Now with me, since I had been without women for so long, and was discovering them at last after so many twists and turns, I felt like an addict who was finally able to get a fix. Anything about women, their bodies, their loves, became an obsession to me, arousing my curiosity, my greed, my urge to investigate and conquer. Have you ever made love in a threesome?"

"No, not really. The only time I came near it, the third one put her clothes back on and split."

"To me, it was a real discovery. I had never done it with two men, but I have a fine, exciting recollection of two girls I met at Deauville. They were two gorgeous models, who had come down to do the fashion show at the casino. I was there at the tail end of a kind of pseudo-seminar, the kind where you're bored stiff and drink too much to forget that you're wasting your time. I knew one of the girls, and knew she wasn't averse to a bit of girl-partying once in a while. We had a drink together at the bar, and then I suggested we carry on with a bottle of Dom Pérignon up in my room. We were feeling very happy, not drunk, just with a slight edge on, and I was ready to go over the edge.

"Let's call the girls Sym and Ingrid. Sym and I had already exchanged a few glances that lent themselves to no misunderstanding. She showed that she liked me, and the sight of these two superb creatures in my room, lying on one of the beds, like two languid felines, gave me a rosy outlook about the future of the human race, beauty, the right to live one's loves, and what have you. We were into those big empty speeches that are fed by alcohol. Ingrid had rested her head on Sym's hip. I sat down near her and petted her hair. She was as blonde as Sym was brunette. I leaned over her and lightly touched her lips. She smiled, and I went on. She let herself be kissed, then started to return my kiss—at first awkwardly, like all women who are used to men's hard, muscular lips that devour and crush. But she caught on soon enough to the wonderful feeling of softer, more tender sensations, the tongue not driven into the other's palate like a prick, or swinging wildly around your own tongue, which gets thrown by such febrile agitation that goes too fast to let you have any chance to savor it."

"That's one of the things gay guys say they have against feminine types, if memory serves me—that their tongues are too soft and too mushy."

"Well, one thing is sure, a kiss for us is not the same as it is for men. From the very first contact, what a difference between them and us! Men kiss our mouths the way they kiss us elsewhere or anywhere. In a word, they're fucking, whereas we rather go gathering the honey from the lips, and teeth, and the tongue of our partner, slowly, at length, the better to savor each contact, each sensation."

"What happened then? What did you do with Sym? What was she up to while you were making time with her little friend? That's where my imagination gets lost. I have the feeling that in any threesome, one always gets screwed —I mean, left out in the cold.

"Let me explain. It's not a question of morals, or taboo, or breaking the rules. If I'm against threesomes, it's for three reasons:

"First of all, it seems to me it's quite absorbing enough to make love *properly* to another woman without having your mind and body distracted by a third party. Physical love has to be built up with movements, caresses, kisses, whispers, moans, groans, rubbings, by sound, by touch, and by taste. You get out of your skin, you're laid bare, nerves and flesh, the other one has become the universe. There is little time, in lovemaking, fully to taste that body facing you, that body against you, to magnify it. My mind, and head, and senses are just not up to taking off, swinging around, splitting toward a third body. By taste, I'm a monogamist for that time being.

"Or else, the third person is often just there to spice things up. The pepper you throw in to heighten the dulled sauce of a body you already know all too well. A kind of living dildo coming to the rescue of insufficient imagination, inadequate ardor. Not my cup of tea! I would like to be something else in life than a twig of thyme or a clove of garlic! I have too much respect for women to make one of them play the role of a ribbon you tie around a package to make it more attractive.

"Finally, and especially, I find that making love without any love in it is just doing nothing; and to make three-way love, for all three to be in love with one another—no, there's just one too many. To stay in unison in double harness is difficult enough. In triple, it's impossible."

"I don't know," Sylvie replied. "It seems to me rather that it's a question of ambience, and also of complicity.

"I imagine that Sym had desperately wanted to make love with Ingrid, but up to then hadn't dared. I was the primer, the artificer fallen from heaven. We both wanted to teach that ravishing creature what loving women was all about, that was all there was to it. As I told you, it developed quite simply. After a bit, we were all stripped. Sym put her arms around Ingrid and I watched them play with each other, as I knelt at the edge of the bed. It was splendid: these two dreamlike cover girls just for me alone, for my own intoxicated pleasure! Both of them had very slim bodies, with high small breasts, round and smooth rumps, long thighs, and delicate hands with bright red nails. Even with their hair awry, their lipstick long since devoured in kisses, their mascara running and giving them dark circles under the eyes, they were still a delight to the eye, a voluptuousness to the soul. Everything was sweetness, loving-kindness. We didn't have to force Ingrid.

"She was a tamed doe, palpitating without restraint. Then Sym went down on her. I in turn put my lips on Ingrid's. I softly caressed her nipples, looking down from time to time in wonder at Sym's dark head of hair, through which could be divined a blond moss, like a sun breaking through to the underbrush. Ingrid came against my lips.

I drank in her groans, and then her cries. She was wild, twisting and shaking in our arms, so we found it hard to keep her on the bed, which was too narrow for our three intertwined bodies. We slipped off onto the carpet. Afterward, there wasn't the slightest embarrassment. We all smiled at one another. She said, 'That was beautiful.' She was conscious of what that moment meant to us all. She didn't say 'That was good,' or 'I liked that,' which would have spoiled everything. No, it was beautiful, these three women making love. After that, well—I began to kiss Sym. We made love to each other at the same time, caressing each other under Ingrid's marveling eyes. She kept repeating, 'How beautiful it is!' We made love to each other without brutality, only with playful caresses, without actually possessing each other, by unspoken agreement. It was important to preserve the sweetness, the tenderness. Our coming was practically all in the mind, yes, a wonderful recollection . . .

"The second time I found myself with two other women, they were a couple of girls I had met on vacation. The thing played itself out almost the same way. I don't think it's ever much different from that when you've got three women making love. Wild-haired dykes riding each other as they talk dirty for stimulation, with their eyes popping out of their heads and spit drooling out of their mouths, that's something that belongs in X-rated movies, and I've never seen anything like it except in jerkoff houses."

"Oh, I adore porno films, Sylvie. The stories are always so pitiful and the actors so lousy-looking that I laugh my head off in my seat. Since I usually go to them with a girl friend I drag along because I can't get anyone else to go with me, she keeps shoving her elbow into me for fear one of the single spectators will make me shut up by hitting me with what he's holding in his hand. I think they're a lot more fun than westerns! What a show those frantic cocks are! And, Lord, how little imagination they show!

All built around the two great male fantasies: the blow job to end all blow jobs and the lady getting on top and humping him (Texas-style, some call it). All they want is to be taken, to be dominated, to play the passive partner . . ."

"Well, I don't say I don't like to see one once in a while, but they get so monotonous, and really you never learn anything new. Especially about the way two women love each other. You can see that the arrangement and the direction are all done by men and for men. The movements are wrong, the caresses are ridiculous, meaningless. And when the girls pretend to be coming, it's all you can do to keep from yelling 'Fake!' "

"You know, my friend Joëlle is an actress, and once we went up to see a friend of hers who runs a cutting and dubbing studio that specializes in porno. After all, everybody has to make a living!

"It was a madhouse, from the minute we walked in. Two young women film cutters were sitting at their Moviolas, looking disgusted, and mumbling, 'More hard-ons, more hard-ons, enough already!'

"But upstairs was where the real fun began. There were three open cutting rooms, with men and women cutters calling to each other from one room to the next: 'Hey, come and look at this one! What a hunk!' And they'd all burst out laughing, delighting in their work.

"What I wanted to see was where they dubbed the voices in. Unfortunately, it was noon already, and the actors had gone to lunch—to wash out of their mouths the tastes of all those gaping cunts and dribbling cocks they had been lending their voices to all morning.

"But the sound-effects man was there. Ah, the sound-effects man, Sylvie! That was one of my great moments at the movies! Try to imagine a typical old grandfather type sitting with the tools of his trade spread out before him: a pair of keys, two pieces of hinged wood (to simulate closing doors), a doormat, and a washbowl full of water. The scene he was looking at wound up with a fellatio. Big close-up of the lady's mouth going to work. And turning, I saw the sound-effects man conscientiously sucking his thumb, faster and faster, to match the rhythm on the screen. Like a big pink baby, he was following each move to synchronize every gulp in the throat and swish of the tongue. And then it was over. The sound-effects man starts to rumple his clothes as the man is getting dressed on the screen; the actor goes out, slams the door, and the wood clacks. In the garden, there was now a naked woman. And the sound-effects man was at it again, kissing the palm of his own hand noisily, and then the man lay down, and the naked broad straddled him. The sound-effects man yells to the dubbing director:

" 'What are they fucking on?'

" 'How should I know?'

"Cut. Now you see the lady's knees and then her legs.

" 'Oh, shit!' the sound-effects man yells. 'They're on grass. Let's go back to the top.'

"And the film reels backward, just as entertaining, and then the lady squats on the guy again, as the sound-effects man rubs his feet over the doormat, now simulating their bed of grass. And then, as the lady goes into a little trot tempo, the sound-effects man dips his hands in the water and, by squeezing them together, treats us to a delightful concert of very suggestive suction sounds, in time to the lady's trot and then the gallop she rides into. All of it nothing but illusion! Men are perfectly satisfied with such illusions. They have their faked porno movies, their wild hard-core books written by old codgers in bedroom slippers who use pen names like Alick de Mycock, and then the whores that they pay off at a street corner, or in some sordid hotel room, or even at the George V (but the make-believe is always the same). But all they get their ecstasy from is a wind-up doll that says 'Pay me,' instead of 'Papa!' or 'Mama!'—a sad kind of 'happiness.'

"Men like to be fooled; they live on illusions. How many of them are aware of it, and how many, being aware, brush the evidence violently aside, because 'it's easier that way'?"

"We're not that way, Elula, quite obviously. A lesbian whorehouse would go broke. Look at how many gay bathhouses there are. Nothing like that on our side . . ."

"Oh, but there is—in the minds of men! Every so often someone (almost always a man) comes and whispers something to me about a Turkish bath full of gorgeous lesbian houris. I just smile. Because whenever anything new in the lesbian or feminist line is started in Paris, you can be sure I'm the first to know about it. Well, I can assure you that there is no such thing, nor is there likely to be, in the sense that they imagine it, that is to say, a kind of smoke-filled pickup center where you could go down on some strange woman surrounded by fragrant mists . . . But let's get back to your second three-headed party. You said the other two lived together. So things may have been different. Did they pick you up the way straight couples pick up a swinging single, to serve as the ketchup on their roast?"

"No, not at all. They were a little couple from Limoges. Two darling little schoolteachers, twenty-two and twenty-five. They adored each other—or, rather, were trying to find out whether what they were doing was right, whether they were overlooking movements or caresses that might make them even happier, for they had started their liaison as virgins four years before. They came right out and told me that after a few days. I hardly make a prudish impression on people, you know, so they dare say the most difficult things to me. I watched them make love to each other, and then I made love to the prettier one. The other meanwhile was fondling me, but her eyes were wide open and taking everything in. They got a big kick out of it, but I didn't. I wasn't there for my own enjoyment, but wanted them to get all they could out of it, so I really had to concentrate.

"But they were so happy, in each other's arms, like two little kitties licking their chops. I tiptoed out after one last smile at them. And the next morning I was off again. They wrote me a very nice letter, saying that thanks to me they knew they were accomplished lesbians and that never again would they know any bodies other than each other's, since all women are alike and they had found perfect happiness together. For my part, I've never been that optimistic about couples staying together forever. I believe in passionate alliances, but I also believe that time is a great eroder. And while I may admire couples that can overcome it, I can't say that I envy them. My love for women is too violent and ardent for me to be the woman in one single life. After my Abidjan newspaperwoman I made up for all the women I'd been missing. For years, I really cruised around picking up trade like a guy. I seduced them, I screwed them, and then if some other pretty heart happened by . . ."

"But what about your earlier safaris?"

"You mean my forays into the world of men? Oh, yes, I still bagged a few of them . . . I'm not a girl to ponder over things too much, you know. It never occurred to me, after I'd made love to a woman, to look at myself in the mirror when I got up and see if I had changed. No, I remained just the same as I had been. It was just that my body had wanted something different.

"I didn't try to philosophize about it, or try to analyze whether or not I was a lesbian, or whether or not I was bisexual. I met women I liked and I made love to them, and when a guy caught my fancy—well, why not? Only the men seemed gradually to be getting less and less frequent in my bed. The fact was, I didn't have the *yen* for them anymore. It wasn't a matter of repulsion—after all I'd done for so many years, that would have been ridiculous, wouldn't it?—but just more and more indifference to what they had to offer and what they could do for me.

"And then I came back to France ten years ago, and I met Andrée, and then Catherine and Marie, whom you've met. I loved them. Especially Marie. She was beautiful, intelligent, and utterly charming. We lived together for three years. In the business I'm in now, traveling all over Europe all the time, my Paris apartment is just a place where I make slightly longer stopovers. And in those circumstances it's hard to have a solid relationship. Your partner has to have an awful lot of patience, as well as confidence. You know, it's not easy being a sailor's woman!

"I don't ever screw men anymore, and I don't imagine I ever will again. I've known enough of them to feel I know them all. I know everything that they can do for me. And I also know what women can do for me. Men have never brought me any feeling of growth. With them, I never experienced that wonderful feeling of 'sisterhood,' of understanding and total complicity. Even their lovemaking, their sexual apparatus, which I didn't find distasteful, never completely sent me. I could never grow lyrical about the glories of a big fat cock, whereas a woman's face, her rounded knee, the dimple in the small of her back can make me delirious.

"Yet that doesn't mean I'm hostile to men. Why hold it against them? They were born males and can't do anything about it. They may hold no interest at all for me anymore on a sexual level, but they can still be interesting human beings. We're always accusing them of being chauvinistic toward us, so I don't think we ought to be toward them."

"I'll buy that, Sylvie! There's no reason for us to be harpies waving our fists and shouting stupid useless slogans like 'Off with their balls!' or 'All men to the gas ovens!' There are much more important things for us to get them to admit."

"Such as?"

"You don't need twenty-five volumes or fake medical jargon to state what everyone can see but is only beginning to be aware of: When a child is born, still dripping with the fluid in which it has lived and bathed for nine months, it is placed on its mother's belly. The first hands that wash it, diaper it, feed it, are women's hands. The first face it sees, looking down at it, is its mother's. She's the one who nurses it or feeds it. In a word, just everything all about it, from birth to first consciousness, is *female*.

"Therefore, all your big psychoanalysts after due consideration come to the deep conclusion that it is perfectly normal for man to be attracted by a woman, who has mothered him from his earliest perception. That attraction to the opposite sex is natural and undeniable. But where does that leave us women? As Françoise Paramel correctly points out in her book *La Femme homosexuelle* [The Homosexual Woman], who was it who diapered and cradled and fed us? Our fathers? Only on rare occasions. And who guided our first steps? Our uncles?

"Who bathed us and powdered us, and kissed our little hands, or bellies, or footsies? Our grandfathers?

"So why shouldn't a little girl be equally attracted by the mother-woman? Why is what is normal for a little boy be abnormal for a little girl? In order for woman to fulfill her destiny, which is to conjoin with a man for *procreation*, she has to break company with that womanly world which he can go right on enjoying. Like a queen bee, she has to leave the hive in order to swarm, and go off somewhere and lay a little male and pamper him. She has to forsake her original homosexuality in order to become what is expected of her: a heterosexual. The woman is the one who has to make that whole trip to bridge the difference, all by herself, with no other companion than the first doll she got as a toy. A pretty girl doll to pet and love, the better for us to know how to love one another, before we are cruelly driven out of the female universe. Why, then, aren't little boys given a doll to play with instead of toy soldiers?

"No, we're the ones who get tea sets, and cooking ranges, and sewing boxes, to get us familiar right away with what is supposed to be our natural place in life. One New Year's Day I saw the horrible sight of a little three-year-old girl whose Christmas present had been an almost life-sized baby carriage with a big baby in it. She was crossing the street alongside her mother. Barely steady on her little legs, hardly strong enough to push the pram that was too heavy for her, her face was as serious as could be, imbued with her responsibilities. I could see the awful projection of what she would be at twenty, with a real baby in her carriage as she trod heavily in an advanced state of pregnancy. And at sixty, she'd be pushing a grocery cart, dragging along on legs deformed by the varicose veins she had earned in loyal homemaking service. When did she have time to live, that little girl who thought she was playing with her doll, when all the time she was just being programmed and conditioned for the rest of her life?

"We lesbians are the naysayers, the lazy ones, the rebelling queen bees who refuse to forsake the shores of our smooth skins, our secret softnesses, our mutual surrenders. And why should it be that men are allowed to go on wallowing in the female universe, while we have to go looking elsewhere to see if we can find where the men are?"

"There's still a long way to go before things change and society develops . . . How much has to be written and said! I, for one, wouldn't have the courage to take on that mountain of prejudices, false truths, calumnies, and condescending sneers . . ."

"You're painting a slightly dark picture, you know. There are some women who have become aware and some men who have started thinking. Not every one of them is a poor puerile male who only knows how to brandish his penis as if it were a scepter, the axis of the world and the dong of God the Father Himself! I think we have to talk, to write, to tell about endless women, because no two of us have come to our lesbianism or found ourselves in the same way. I'm impressed with your life, Sylvie, because it's such a slap in the face to all the dullards who keep telling me, 'Oh, you've only had one man in your life. You can't know.' "

"Well, maybe my problem was that I had too many. They'd say I had become a lesbian out of surfeit. How silly can they be?"

* * *

Danièle, Joëlle, and our hostesses were coming up the stairs with a bag full of shellfish and crustaceans. The house was filled with aromas of garlic and saffron; my little Pinscher, exhausted from the walk, was panting and snorting like a little sea lion.

It was time to sit down at the table. Once again, the ladies of the house had concocted new wonders for us.

There were six women here.

Two little girls were playing in the yard.

Each of us loved the one who was with us, the one who, tonight, in our arms, would listen to the wind coming up, right along with the tide, toward our windows that opened onto the stars.

We were simply six happy lesbians.

ANNE-MARIE

"Anne-Marie, look, won't you ever learn to dress decently or make yourself look good? No daughter of mine should be seen in jeans like those. And your bra? Why don't you want to wear a bra? You'll see what your bosom looks like when you're thirty."

My bosom . . . Why talk about something that doesn't exist? More like a case of acne that just left me with two largish pimples. Call those tits? Two little dark points, that pop out a little when I make an effort or feel especially excited. That, and nothing more. Hardly what you'd call another Lollobrigida or Loren—just plain, flat Anne-Marie.

Am I pretty? No.

Am I homely? I don't really know.

I've often been struck by the somewhat mad look you see in artists' self-portraits. If I were a painter and painted myself, my eyes would have that look, disquieting in the steadiness of the black, piercing, shiny pupils. The look of a bird of prey.

And my skinny, almost fleshless neck, and my little pointed head with its crew-cut flat hair that makes a dark helmet around my face with its overlong nose, overthin lips, and overbearing chin.

I'm an ambiguous character, huddled before the crackling fire in my room. My eyes closed, I can still hear my mother's voice: "Anne-Marie, do fix yourself up . . ."

> Before woman, God created man,
> For before creating a marvel
> He had to try a first draft . . .

wrote Voltaire.

Perhaps I fall somewhere between the two. Between the blueprint and the finished product, neither fully man nor fully woman, neither totally rough nor completely polished.

I've had enough of this, living like a plant, or a stone, or an insect to be brushed away and crushed.

Within my ordinary, flat, wiry body, there is my soul, my bubbling blood, my weeping heart, my gut crying out. I want to be loved. I want to love. I am alone. Alone on my heath, with my scruffy vegetation, my rocky soil. The wind outside is blowing and my sheep are restlessly baaing in the pen, off to the left side of my hut, the heart side. My sheep are my love; mine is a life beyond normal conventions, but one that allows me not to have to hide my predilections, lets me live as I please, and say so. It is a life that permits me to maintain within myself my gift for being happy and the rage to live that goes with it.

But for now I am all alone, the nights are long, and it will be a long winter. Before springtime, no chance of my escaping from the plateau here. But when the flocks go back up to pasture, I'll turn my animals over to Rodrigo, sling my bag over my shoulder, filled with its rock-hard cheeses, and go off to Roanne to bring them to Agnès. I'll give those milk stones—as others might give moonstones or stones more precious still—to the woman I love.

Agnès, sweet, gentle Agnès, kept me with her all night long that time her husband "went up to Paris." Agnès, of the heavy body, mature, languorous, voluptuous, wild lover-woman, perverse mistress. I, the smooth-skulled little shepherd, grazed upon her, took suck from her like a little fawn. I am dreaming of her before the fire, shivering a bit (with a chill? or desire?) and escaping into time, the time before her, the *times* before her, rather: the short eternity of my thirty-two years in which I had so many different guises, galloping along or stumbling, ambling peacefully or trotting, rarely happy, rarely for long. Happiness? Just sand that all too quickly runs out between my fingers.

How am I made? What kind of two-sided brain do I have, what kind of asymmetrical heart in which the blood flows red, then black, now out, now in, utterly unpredictable? Why can I never ever be satisfied with the moment that is? Baudelaire always wanted to be everywhere except the very place he happened to be. What I always want is love—yet the minute I sense I'm going to be loved, I run away, preferring still to suffer in my loneliness . . .

Maybe the first time I was really happy was when I got a bicycle for my grammar-school graduation. My thighs, wiry already, and taut, squeezed the seat so tightly—I was unconsciously rubbing myself against the leather seat, making it into my first lover.

As for boys, I wanted none of them. Besides, they didn't seek me out. At ten, we were rivals at marbles; at fifteen, in pickup soccer games; while the girls were swooning during the crazy tangos at the village dances. But I can't remember a single suggestive gesture, meaningful look, or wandering hand. I'm just not the kind of girl that gets ravished—or even gets lusted after.

And yet, there was Jacques, who came along after a long arid period. Was it just the thirst for love? It was less than that. Just a desire to give in, to have the warmth of a body to remember. I could no longer stand falling asleep hugging a corner of the mattress in my arms, the way unhappy children hang onto their teddy bears.

Then the idiot went around bragging about how well he'd fucked me, and how appreciative of it I was. What an egotistical jerk to think I'd slept with him because I liked him . . .

God, was that ever repulsive and disgusting! His warmish rod shoving into the hollow of my crotch, his hurried breathing, his awkward hip movements, and rough hands on my shoulders; I turned my head away to avoid his tobacco breath. I panted a little to try to excite him just to get him to finish with it, and finally he rolled over on his side after grunting like a lumberjack and then yelling a shrill discordant yell—it was enough to turn anyone off.

I got up, went to the bathroom, and sat on the bidet, feeling ridiculous, sticky, and wet. I would have liked to vomit, sweat, piss, anything to get all the semen out of me in any way I could. I shivered. Never again! No, never again! Better to rub against the corner of my mattress, better to shed bitter tears, better to live with my overwhelming love for a woman I would never dare approach—but never, never again would I have a man.

It was in Lyons. An electronics seminar that was just fascinating! Nothing but men around the horseshoe-shaped table. And I was bored stiff. I was listening distractedly. I was doodling S-shaped lines, curves that worked themselves into hips and breasts. I couldn't keep from thinking of the girl I'd seen that morning, in her orange T-shirt, tight-fitting jeans, black boots, very short blond hair, and pretty, oh so pretty . . . a walking invitation to misconduct. I had remained motionless, entranced, half-hidden by a newspaper kiosk. She was waiting for another woman, who came to join her, and looked like her, with that arrogant ease of women who know they are pretty, visibly satisfied with her physical superiority.

It didn't matter at all to me that they might see me reflected in the hardware window, paralyzed, openmouthed, looking somewhat retarded, my chest half-exposed in the opening of my tailored shirt, my titlets suddenly sprung to life, but alas! not life enough to turn anyone on . . .

How many times have I devoured passing women in the same way, penetrating their eyes, violating their bodies . . . That little redhead at the Provence trailer camp, who never seemed to notice me, never became aware of the fact that I looked at her or how insistently I did it. What extraordinary fulfillment I got from the impunity of my own gaze: I could literally eat her with my eyes, any way I wanted; all of a sudden, I had become invisible.

But during this electronics seminar, every man's eyes transmitted the identical message: Dash-dot-dot-dash—*"Voulez-vous coucher avec moi ce soir?"* in the lyrics of one of that season's hit songs.

As usual, my movements and my words gave me away. My eyes betrayed me, it was too evident how I ducked when the men became too specific in their conversation. Why did I have to go to so much trouble to hide the fact? Yes, I love women—and why couldn't I yell it at them? Sometimes, it's like a great burning river that wants to stream out of my mouth, a bright flame bursting from my lips: *"Women . . . Women . . ."*

The first girl I ever touched I had already loved so much in silence; she was so beautiful, so diaphanous, so melodious, how could I say what day and under what exact circumstances I first got down on my knees before her? It seems as if I spent my whole adolescence on my knees like that, holding her hand, at times kissing it lightly with the kind of veneration one has for the relics of saints.

I finally got to love her completely after months of idolizing her and gently caressing her ankles, her knees, her thighs; then there was a patient, cautious, almost imperceptible rise, a slow invasion that left her defenseless: How can one stop a gesture that is barely more daring than the previous one, that goes only a fraction beyond where it was yesterday? . . . At what point can one say "Stop"? What frontiers can be declared the impassable limits? There was my soft, sliding hand, stroking her gently, spending hours over that newly accessible spot, discovering with utter delight a smoother skin grain that turned into an unbelievably fine, impalpable silk, warmer and warmer, moister and moister, until finally I bumped into a tiny strip of material, stubborn and unyielding, then days and days for my palm to remain over the moist cloth, my heart beating before the unknownness of a vagina other than my own, that one of my own that I did not know, that I had never been into, had never explored.

The day when I finally spread aside that thin cloth and ran my fingers into a stiff, almost flat fur, I got a disagreeable wet feeling that disgusted me. I knew nothing of the flowing, I was totally ignorant of love, its waiting, its pleasure, its manifestations. I could not recognize the dew, the rain, the lakes, and the ponds. All I got out of it was the stickiness. But I overcame my disgust, and finally I was rewarded by her muffled moans, her trembling; she let her head roll over on the back of the armchair before which I was kneeling.

This was the discovery of orgasm brought about by my hands, the intoxication of conquest, of subjugation. She was caressing my head that lay against her thigh. From her skin there came up an aroma I had never smelled, heady, sensual, that made me forget all of my initial reluctance. My fingers by now were habituated, no longer hesitant but instinctive; they let themselves be guided by the swells of her belly, wandering for endless hours in the humid bushes, the moist velvet, the drenched petals.

The discovery of woman, or, in other words, of love. For they are synonyms. Love means only loving women. Each one and all of them.

Woman . . . Woman . . . Every time I write that word, I feel as if the paper is beginning to burst into flames, as if my pen cannot hold still.

And the memory of Joy. Will I ever dare to write her? A woman who was not especially attracted to women and who was still too young to know whether she preferred men. I never mentioned my desire to her, the urge I had to make love to her. We talked and talked for nights on end, smoking too many Gauloises, drinking too many beers. Joy, with her stumbling French, the hesitating words that I felt like plucking off her lips so they wouldn't bruise themselves as they fell. Tomorrow I'll write her.

Tonight I'm curled up in my sheets. I could have come long and well if that idiot of a voice hadn't suddenly started to yell louder and louder to me that there was no one else there beside me, inside me. What I would have liked was a voice that ran its cool hands over my skin and closed my eyes; but all there was, was the cold. In a hundred years, I'll still be in love with women I have seen on the street, alone in my bed, able to clasp nothing but emptiness.

That harvest girl, what a beautiful student! Why couldn't I get up from the table, walk around to her side, bite into her plump fleshy lips, touch the heavy tits under her white smock? She and the boy went out to get the mare. I was walking behind them so as to inhale her smell, to drink in the beauty of that body she was going to give to him. They couldn't see me. They had their arms around each other and didn't even remember I was there. When they made love to each other, I listened; I touched my body that was overflowing with jealousy and desire.

What I am is a beardless male with two little tits. Sometimes I tell myself I bet I'd like it if I were normal. Actual virility may be easier to take on than a pair of imagined balls. But if I had them, maybe I wouldn't love women! So let's forget it. I'll stay the way I am, famished, but with a headful of women, all women, women always in the background, hidden behind every word, every thought, every sound.

Anyway, what difference would it make if there were a woman in my life? What difference, except maybe even more exasperation, more frustration, or, on the other hand, very quickly losing interest, the way it was with Ruja.

First there was the joy of possessing a woman, as private property, a doll of inflated flesh, available every night in my bed. To feel beneath my fingernails that soft tapestry of her vagina, my fingers bumping into the little round ball, caressing its small crack so similar to a mouth, the opening to her uterus, to lick her armpits, the crook of her elbows, the gold of her groin, to wait patiently, laying circular siege with my lips and my tongue before finally assailing the little flower at the tip of her brown triangle, to make her moan, make her cry out, on and on. Meanwhile, the Spanish housemaids in the neighboring rooms knock on the walls because nighttime is the time for sleep, and in the morning Madame will not approve of the deep circles under Consuelo's or Conchita's eyes.

Ruja, who could make my taut body vibrate like a bow, in an almost unbearable spasm of pleasure, bordering on pain, although the words I spoke, along with my wild eyes, terrified her.

Is it because the reality turned out to be less than what I had dreamt? I ended up hating this girl whose flesh and foreign hand had taken hold of me. Suddenly, the sky darkened and the storm broke. I told her to get out, to leave Paris. I could no longer stand the city, its closed-in people, its women, even the most beautiful of them, never seen any way but running, like crazed ants—stenographers, salesgirls, students, always with worried eyes, with dull, dead faces. Only the concierges remained adorable. The coed I was then made them laugh, even if at times the girls I brought home from my midnight hunts cried out a little too violently, talked a little too loud. To the concierges, it was quite simple. I often ate with them in their little lodges, after giving them a hand with the stairs, or helping them polish the railing. They never mentioned these one-night women to me, women that I was going through like tissues that you use once and throw away. That was the period when I was so horribly like a guy.

How did I do it? How did I, Anne-Marie, ever get to have that many girls?

And now, here alone, crying out on my heath, could I still do it? Would I know how? I was twenty. My stupid daring, my thoughtless approaches paid off. I had women; they came to me, as fascinated by me as by a snake. I spoke to them of making love and what they heard was "I love you." I wove a poisonous web around them and they came, hypnotized, right into it. I could feel the fear that lay just beneath their desire. I wore myself out making them come; sweating in winter, drenched in summer, my tongue burning and almost paralyzed. When morning broke, I wanted to be alone, to lie by myself in my too narrow bed. I wanted to rub myself against the sheets with their odors and traces, so as to recall the lust of the night before, the lust that in my eyes transformed them, spun haloes over them, and made a beauty of the lowliest of tramps.
And here I am now, dreaming of pure love, caressing beautiful, faraway women that exist only for me.
Is a woman really much more than a fine idea? Is a woman really also sex and skin?
When suddenly did women start to do without me, to rebel against me, to shun my bed? Was it only the fact that I was eighteen that they liked? Were they simply enjoying making it with a kid, a strange little page who talked feverish, revolutionary words to them and made them smile?
Someplace within me, there must still be some kind of potential for seduction, even if it's atrophied. I would like a woman, a woman. I would tell her how beautiful she is, beautiful as a wild filly, beautiful as a little lost lamb, beautiful as a sunlit prairie . . .
I would like to write a love letter—to any woman. To Joy—to ask her whether she honestly never understood the

meaning of my fevered eyes. To Agnès—to beg her once more to let me breathe in her milky, very soft breasts which my palms could form into any shape that I wished.

The winter will soon be over. And I am here, my mind wavering. Janis Joplin and Mahler, worn thin by too many trips around my lousy record player. That's what I'll replace first. Not my little car; I care less about its rattling and creaking and more about Joplin's soul-shattering voice —now stilled.

I riffle through dress catalogs. All those women on parade, frozen in equivocal positions, with unreal movements, impossible balance, stereotyped smiles. I would like to send for a free sample of their hair or their skin, to find out whether they are as soft as in my dreams, as bright as they seem.

Choosing sheep was just a return to my sources, daughter of peasants that I am. The city suffocates me with its women. Here I can breathe. My boots are heavy with clay, my mackinaw moist with the haze, my gray cloth hat is the very one that Agnès's husband must have worn when he went hunting—it's all that I have left of her . . .

Roanne is so far and yet so near . . . She was so amused to see such a wild little shepherd having dinner at Jean and Maria Janin's, my great black eyes devouring her. I had not said a word to her. I answered the other guests only in monosyllables when they commented on my return to the land, my return to my roots. Roots, my eye! My only roots are in my head. Soft arms and smooth legs, tentacles of perfumed flesh that search through my brain, tearing away strips of gray matter, a kaleidoscope of tits and dark pubes.

My ovine odor must persist even when I am curried and scoured, when I swap my mackinaw for the embroidered Afghan sheepskin I bought in Petticoat Lane; even though the sheep may be Pakistani, the smell is the same.

When liqueurs were served, Agnès came over and sat by me.

"Are you planning to be in town long?"

I was dying to bite her mouth, dig my fingers into her neck where a pale-blue vein was pulsing. I wanted to tear away her golden silk jellaba and ravish her warm, perfumed body.

Oh, the things I said to her then about the thousand and one nights, about woman, about eunuchs, and the caliph, and my wild belly-damsel's heart! I think it was the sangría that had gone to my head. Agnès's husband got into the conversation. Why is it that the first thing men always want to try to find out is why I'm not looking for a man? And how do I know? I'm really fed up with always having to try to explain that, when I have no idea myself.

He went off full of smugness; purring with respectability and self-satisfaction. He, after all, was well balanced. He had a wife he screwed, children he raised, a business he ran—all the trappings of a normal life.

But I don't have a thing. No money, no wife, a crazy profession, just a profound need to *live* before I die.

When all the others had left, Jean, Maria, and I still stayed on a while to talk. Then I helped Maria wash up and put away the leftovers. Jean was smoking his pipe, rearranging the recordings that had been left out of their liners, and emptying the overflowing ashtrays. I felt that I was being let in on a privileged moment of family life, the sweet quiet, the tacit understanding, with dogs barking in the distance, the French door wide open into the terrace with its lilacs.

I felt I was the little girl I had never been: pretty, with barrettes on my hair and red ribbons, and a little fox terrier that ran around with me in the garden, taking vacations at the beach and building sand castles, going to my first real party, having my first beau . . .

I finally turned in. I felt quiet and peaceful. And I thought of Agnès again. One more to add to my list of unreachables . . .

She came back the next day. To return a book Maria had lent her. My hostess whispered to me that that was just "an excuse." She all but shoved me right into Agnès's arms, and left us alone. I was paralyzed, my tongue stuck to my palate. Only my eyes were alive—and they spoke volumes for me. Agnès eyed me with amused curiosity, as if I were some strange animal.

"She's a great lay," Jean declared, when he heard she was there after he got home. "Always ripe for anything new. You're the latest thing to catch her fancy."

Here I am, at my fireside, writing this. For whom? And why? I can recall bits of dialogue, fragments of faces, outbursts of my own endless monologue, and the nauseating recollection of Jacques, and Agnès's milky blondness.

But who the fuck cares anything about my ideal, my love for Woman, my profession? Who gives a damn about me? All I am is a hungering cry for women that can't satisfy its desire, always meeting shadows that vanish before me.

Ideal women—idealized women—you whom I've loved for not having touched, you whom I've lusted after for not being able to get near . . .

Tonight I am everything. The whipping dominatrix and the frightened slave, the woman triumphant in her conquest and the fulfilled submissive female, the breathless sweetheart and the bitch in heat. I am all women and all lesbians, I am the vein that pulses in the hollow of the throat, the corner of the moist-lipped mouth, I am the dizzying cleavage between the breasts and the shadow deep between the thighs, I am the hard hand and the soft tongue, I am ember-hot eyes and muffled cry. I am all of this— filled with womanness—and I am alone.

Perhaps Agnès, because she tamed me without trying to put me into a cage, because she is unavailable when her husband is home in Roanne, because she is a woman, a real one, full of scents and sounds, because, when I come into her, inside her deep-sea grotto the air comes in and then goes out, just like the ocean at high tide, and as it withdraws leaves behind a thousand sighs that vibrate into my heart.

Agnès . . . When the snow and the rain are over, I will go to Roanne, and bring you my milk stones.

ÉLODIE

After ten years' good and faithful services in cabarets the world over, at the first visible wrinkle, the first little sag of her small apple-shaped breasts, Élodie retired from the stage, saying farewell to the spangles, the dusty dressing rooms, and the smoke-filled nightclubs.

Élodie, who had been known for her acrobatic stripteases, bought a small beauty salon on the Left Bank, in the Fifteenth Arrondissement.

I am not one of those militant feminists who proclaim that makeup and careful grooming turn women into a sex object and a commodity of the consumer society, or that ugliness, among women, is a nonexistent notion, or that competitiveness and cattiness surface only when there is an available male on the horizon.

To feel that way is really to give them too much importance! I don't make up, or take care of myself, or have my hair done in order to be appealing to men. I do those things for myself first of all, because I want to be pleased when I look in the mirror, and, beyond that, for other women! Out of respect and love for them, I want to appeal to other women.

So it was when I went to Élodie's salon, and lay stretched on the table, my face covered with various creams and muds, that I had a chance to hear her talk, as her soft, light, skillful hands ministered to me.

The weeks went by, and Élodie little by little let me in on her story. It wasn't easy. In her old profession, she had acquired a mistrust and a reserve that I am all too familiar with. Night people are not generally straightforward: The slightest remark made in that nocturnal atmosphere, with its alcohol, its noises, its mishmash of classes and kinds, bounces back, resounds, gets distorted, and returns to you in some wild new twist, like a boomerang. You have to weigh every word when you work in a milieu where the clowns and practical jokers are not always the people on the stage.

Élodie talked haphazardly, mixing up anecdotes and comments. She talked about her life, and this is what she said.

* * *

I was born in the suburb of La Courneuve—so I'm a real Parisienne, as you can see. I was an only child, in an uncomplicated family. My father was a bookkeeper, and we lived in a nice little house. Mother stopped working when I was born, my parents got along together very well, and still do. They never wanted to have another child and Mother never dressed me in boy's clothes to take the place of the son she didn't have—or at least not so far as I can remember.

I was the one who always wanted to dress up in boy's clothes, not because I felt more at home in them, not at all, because I was never unhappy or ashamed of being who I was, but just to see how people would take to me if I was dressed that way, how they would treat me. It was just a little girl's sort of dare, a signboard I was putting on my back; I wanted to see whether I could shock people, like young people who often go off to political extremes, on the right or left, to create an identity for themselves. I was extremely lesbian, and I wanted the world to know it.

Mother would buy me the slacks I wanted, and shorts, and ties, and cuff links. I think she thought it was cute for her little girl to play soldier, so she was quite willing to help me get into disguise, just as she had bought me cowboy or Zorro outfits when I was smaller.

She didn't see anything wrong with it, and I just went on wearing pants. I was working part-time for an insurance company then. One day, Personnel called me in and said, "You're not properly dressed for the type of work you do." Proper dress for filing papers, indeed! How questionable or scandalous-looking could I seem, in my boy's attire and standing five feet one? For anybody there to take me for a faggot, they would really have to be blind! Anyway, I thought that would be a good time to split from there, because I had no desire to spend the rest of my days at that kind of a job.

To tell the truth, I didn't much know what kind of a job I wanted. After passing my *baccalauréat*, which I did without even trying, I did a little drawing, and thought I might get into advertising. I was pretty good at it. A nice pencil touch, they said. Most often—maybe too often—what I drew was women's bodies, women's faces that I had glimpsed and was re-creating from memory.

Among others, there was a portrait that hung over my bed for the longest time: an imaginary woman behind a curtain of long blond hair that practically hid her body, all the way down to the waist. All you could make out was one dark but enticing eye, one tiny little breast, and one almost virile, determined hand, holding the hair down at shoulder height, as if to keep me from lifting the hair and gazing at her face and chest . . .

I can remember my first sex reaction. It was when I was in primary school at La Courneuve. I must have been eight. I had a crazy crush on a little blond girl, a real doll, who was maybe five or six. She had ringlets and an angel's face. One day the teacher sent me on an errand into her classroom. I was very proud: Only good students were picked for such errands. I went into the room, and the minute I saw her sitting there in the front row, my heart stopped beating. I just stood speechless, motionless, and what I had come there for completely flew out of my head.

"How stupid can you be!" the teacher yelled at me. "Go on back and ask what it was you forgot!"

I don't even remember the name of that pretty little girl; but at the Thursday-afternoon movies, I would plot so I could get to sit next to her. I took her by the shoulders, and put my arm around her, and I was oh, so happy!

It was usual, at school, to have a young "protégée." It worked like a chain reaction. The older girls protected a younger one, who in turn protected one still younger. So, I, too, had an elder protector. She was already beginning to look a little like a grown-up, with breasts and a permanent. I felt at ease with her, but what I wanted was to touch the little one, to pet her, to fondle her.

I was already the way I am now. I love to feel protected, taken care of, but I am just as happy to be the one who does the protecting and caretaking. That's the way it is when you're both active and passive at the same time, in harmony with yourself and uncomplicated.

My first kiss on the mouth was given me by a boy. Or maybe I should say forced on me, for that's what happened! What an awful memory! It was at a neighborhood movie house, one Sunday afternoon. The boys were having fun teasing the girls. I guess they still do that sort of thing. That day one of them got next to me and slipped his tongue into my mouth. It almost made me puke. When I got home, I brushed my teeth at least a dozen times.

I was twelve. And it was about the same time that I had my first affair.

Her name was Raymonde. In our coeducational lycée, I hung around mostly with boys, but that was as far as it went. The problem was that I already felt much too womanly. I was well formed, with breasts just as big as they are now. All right, I'm no Jane Russell—but for a twelve-year-old kid, my boobs were pretty good! Mother bought me the kind of bras that made them stand out; and the minute I was out of the house, I would unhook them, so that no one could see that I had any tits at all.

Raymonde was eighteen. Not very far ahead in her

schoolwork, but right up there on other accounts! Since she was always out dating guys on Thursdays when there was no school, her parents, who both worked, would lock up her clothes so she couldn't go out. All they left her were a dressing gown and a pair of slippers.

I would go and spend Thursday afternoons with her. One day she told me confidentially, "You know, when I read, I play with myself. Have you ever tried doing it?"

"No."

"Well, go ahead, then. Try it. See, this is the way to do it."

She was lying on her bed, with her bathrobe open; her hand was moving slowly, then faster and faster. She was panting, and saying to me, "It feels so good, oh, so good . . . Go ahead, you try, too."

I was petrified and horrified by what I saw. Then she uttered a final sigh, and appeared to have fallen asleep.

I ran away. For two weeks, I didn't go back to see her. And then one fine Thursday, I rang her doorbell again—and that time she taught me how . . .

How exciting our Thursday afternoons became! Her parents might just as well have taken away her bathrobe and slippers too, because she never had them on when we were together.

Was it good? The first time she caressed me, I had a strange, unprecedented feeling, but one that I liked very, very much. Not really an orgasm yet, to be sure. I don't know exactly when the first time was that I came with her, but it was with her, of that I am certain.

After Raymonde, I had other little girl friends, on those Thursday afternoons off from school, between fourteen and eighteen. Manuelle, Nathalie, Beebop, Stéphanie . . . I almost got expelled on account of Stéphanie. We had made a date to meet in the girls' room, during class hours, because we weren't in the same class. A monitor happened in and caught us kissing. She went and told the principal.

My father was called in, but he didn't say a thing about it to me. Not a reproach, not a word. Nor did Mother. They were just fine about it all.

Even today we've never discussed the subject openly. Once, during a meal, when I was telling some cock-and-bull story as a cover for what I had been doing, Papa said to me:

"Look, you know that we know, and I know you know that we know. So don't bother with the cover-up."

That was all there was to it. There's never been a problem, because no one made one out of it. My parents have accepted me as I am and they don't ask me to let them know what I'm doing, so long as I don't create any public scandals and haven't brought any shame on them other than that one incident at school.

School was the place where I did have problems. The boys called me a dirty dyke, because not only did I turn all of them down, but I occasionally got some girl away from one of them.

Well, it's as you've said—not only unfuckable, but in competition with them besides . . . No wonder that men hate us!

Between eighteen and twenty-two, I had intercourse with three fellows.

Why? To find out what it was like, so as not to go to my grave without knowing. I loved women, I was a lesbian, there was no doubt about that, but in order to be even surer of it, I wanted to see what it was like with a guy.

With the first one, it was—nice. Yes, that's the best word for it: nice. He was a little effete, almost effeminate. In fact, all three of the fellows were much alike. I couldn't have done it with a hairy, macho type, a virile gorilla. I'm not very vaginal myself, but rather enjoy being caressed, so this nice little fellow wasn't too demanding for my taste.

The second—can't remember. No, word of honor! At

any rate, it didn't matter at all. He must have been very sweet; a passerby, nameless and inoffensive.

Jacques was the third. He had slept with transvestites. He had told me so, maybe because he knew that I loved women.

He was very cute, with big blue eyes, very thick blond hair that he wore quite long, and fine features, almost like a girl's. We made love nicely, even tenderly.

And then, one day, I don't know how or why it happened, I made him up, dressed him in pantyhose and a nightgown. And we made love—how shall I say?—more excitingly. I knew he was only a boy, he knew he wasn't even in drag, and yet it turned us both on.

From that day forward, we never made love again any way but watching each other. You see what I mean? Shared masturbation, each of us coupling with our own fantasy: my imagining he was a woman, he thinking he had finally turned into one . . .

We got along together very well, fully respected each other's "freedom," and so he thought we ought to get married. I wasn't really against it, but didn't care one way or the other. What good would marriage have done me? I wasn't planning to have any children, and that was the only reason I could see for getting hitched. And besides, at that time, I wasn't all that satisfied with myself, I wasn't ready for permanent arrangements yet.

I have nothing against transvestites, but the idea of marrying one, even if he was only one in his mind, just didn't appeal to me—especially since I didn't want to get married. When I was in show business, I met up with a lot of female impersonators, some of them transsexuals and some just drag queens. Most of them were perfectly fine to work with. But that doesn't mean you'd want to be married to one . . .

* * *

I'm not completely in agreement with Élodie on that

subject. I've had a look at one of those transsexuals, and it wasn't a very pretty sight.

It was in Cannes, at a "specialized" club. The "lady" with her perfect breasts and falsetto voice was in her dressing room, getting made up for her striptease act. I don't remember what brought it on, but she said to me, "Would you like to see my little pussy, darling?"

She was so proud of it! She raised her skirt. I leaned over a piece of ravaged flesh and gazed into the opening that she was spreading with both her hands the better to let me admire it. All I can remember of it was a nauseating odor. After all, this artificial blind alley is not, like a woman's vagina, a living corridor through which the blood of renewal pours out. It is an impasse that must certainly require much more demanding care and maintenance.

It's a simple operation. They make an incision in the pelvis and turn the skin of the penis inward, like an old sock, placing stretchers in that are left there for five to six weeks, during the healing period. It is said to be very painful. If the surgeon has a good gift for landscaping, he is able to form two lips and a kind of mock clitoris with a piece of skin. But as for the subject being able to get any pleasurable sensations from them, I imagine those must exist only in the mind.

Once they've had the operation, it is hard to say what the transsexuals have become. They can't be called lesbians, since they were born males; and yet now they are female, and they still feel attracted to women. What turn of the mind and of their sexual instincts leads these pseudo-females to this? They have themselves amputated in order the better to get close to women, when, as men, they had much greater freedom to do just that. They want to love women like a woman and want also to be loved like a woman . . .

Perhaps what happens is that, once they are rid of that hunk of flesh that hangs so heavy in the minds of men, once they've nearly become women, they become aware of the intrinsic brutality of man and, being hypersensitive to it, take refuge in our arms, they themselves being now disarmed, stripped as it were, disoriented.

But what kind of physical lovemaking can there be between a lesbian and a transsexual? Or even a transvestite? For very often the latter have already mentally castrated themselves and become impotent.

Men who do make love to a transsexual really do fall into the trap that is set for them. The bush before them, more or less convincing according to how good a landscapist the castrating surgeon was, seems to them to be an authentic cunt. How can they know those false labia and clitoris are just fakes? They don't really know what those parts are like, having never been closer to them than the manipulation of a mindless hand. And if the transsexual pretends to be coming, how can they know the orgasm is a falsie just like his/her breasts? Isn't one of the few advantages we have over men the fact that we can put an end to an unproductive embrace by pretending to be fulfilled?

With a lesbian it's different. Knowing that that fake female organ is just an ornament, she steers clear of it. She knows better than to try to give her partner a sensation of enjoyment she knows that "she" can't experience. So I leave it to your imagination how an active lesbian can physically gratify a transsexual . . .

It takes some kind of strange sexual twist and somersault to have yourself amputated to end by being ridden by a lesbian . . .

Most often, however, their relationships remain virtually platonic. They come together through an exchange of great loving-kindness, seeking in caresses and kisses an "aura" of mutual stimulation that is part sweetness, part dismay.

For the lesbian all it can be is one step, a way-station on the path to the real enjoyment of sex.

For the transsexual, on the other hand, it will often be the beginning of an anguish from which there is no escape.

But let's get back to Élodie's story.

* * *

Gil was working as a girl waiter (or *garçonne*) in a night spot, that is, she was a hostess dressed in a tuxedo. She was petite, and despite her masculine outfit not the least bit butch, not at all the "virile gamine." She was a pretty little dark thing, with a pageboy bob and slanted eyes. She was Eurasian.

When the spots went on for the floor show, I saw her leaning against a column, her arms crossed, staring into space. All I could see was she. The show, my friends, Jacques—all had vanished. She just stood there, leaning, and I decided I would get her to see me, get her to love me. Unbelievable how nervy and self-assured I could be about it! I did everything I could to attract her attention, to make her notice me. And I did.

Very quickly we decided we wanted to live together. We were wildly in love. She had broken with the girl she was living with, a barmaid at the place.

But if she moved into our new situation with ease, the same couldn't be said for me.

Of course, I had broken with Jacques, and he had taken it very badly. He made scenes, threatened me, made it impossible for me to carry on with my drawing—in short, my life was shot to hell, except for Gil and me. So it didn't take long for me to head right into a depression. Therapy, psychodrama, tests, and all the rest.

Finally, the psychiatrist who was handling my case, an old patriarch with long white hair that almost came down to his shoulders, a real God-the-Father type and one of the top men in the field, said to me:

"OK, let's cut out all the nonsense. You have to do what you want to do. You want to go and live with that girl? Go ahead and live with her!"

I didn't fight it. No more questions, no more problems. We moved in together. Gil had a little room down near the Gobelins. It wasn't the Hilton. But how happy I was! We were the same age, and in love with each other. What more could you want?

Still, I had to go on earning my living. I couldn't dream of a daytime job. With Gil working at night, we would have had the problem of the night watchman married to the domestic: We would have said hello and good-bye on the stairs, one coming home as the other went out to work.

So, considering that I had a nice-looking body and a pretty face, Gil asked her boss whether I wouldn't be able to fill in for the partner who was about to leave in the acrobatic striptease act that one of her girl friends did.

He called me into his office and simply said, "Hi, kid, take it off." I stripped to the buff.

He just took a glance at me and, as he turned back to his ledgers, he mumbled, "You'll do. You can start in a month."

What a crazy month that was! I had to learn the art from the ground up. Our act was one of the first ones in which two women did something more than just twist their twats and flash their fannies while they took off fake mink coats and other paraphernalia. My partner had to carry me at arm's end, swing me around, we had to assume tableau poses, and do all kinds of acrobatic dances. It was some cram course, believe me!

And then my first night arrived.

It's a helluva tough thing to get out there stripped for the first time in front of an entire audience. Very, very tough. Especially in those days, fifteen years ago, before things got to be the way they are now. No legit actors were appearing nude in stage plays yet.

I have always refused, no matter how high a fee was offered, to go for total nudity. There are limits to everything. And besides, doing the kind of acrobatic numbers we did, having to spread our legs and whatnot, you can see how it would be . . . I had no desire to show off the last intimate stronghold of my love life or have them snatching a look at my most private place . . .

The idea of all those men staring up at me—no, that never really was what bothered me. When you're working, if you're conscientious about it, the work is what you think about.

To feel that I was turning on all the guys out there gave me a lot of professional satisfaction. It just proved I was good at what I was doing. And I did everything I could to feel that I had them going (or should I say coming?). The silence in the room, the tense atmosphere, was very suggestive . . .

Of course, there are always some jerks who sneer or snort or yell out something in more or less questionable taste—but then, there are jerks everywhere, and there always will be.

Who are the quietest? Asians.

I've appeared in Japan, Indonesia, Malaysia, Singapore, as well as all over Europe.

The hottest? The Italians—they're pests, so macho you'd never believe it, but they make one hell of an audience.

The most vulgar? Frenchmen—without any doubt.

The number we did threw the guys for a loop. Of course, they had seen strippers before. And dance numbers with a man carrying his girl partner, too. But one broad carrying another around on one hand, a "weak little woman" who was beautiful, with handsome tits and a fine body, yet showing she was strong as a guy—that got to them. And if carried too far, it actually rubbed them the wrong way in their little feelings of superiority.

. . . You know there're no more whores among strippers than in any other profession. Men may think we'll be easier to lay because we parade around stripped, but that's not true.

Of course, there are some who agree to carry their twosome a little further, at a stag party, if there are enough paying customers. But they don't do any more than two hookers who put on living tableaux for their tricks. It's just as fake. They pretend to be going down on each other, but all they lick is the inside of their thighs, and keep wide of the mark. The men can't see through it. You can be sure that two women, even if they're lesbians and really go for that sort of thing, aren't going to start doing the real thing to each other, and start having real orgasms before a bunch of paying customers.

I never did that kind of thing. I must say I was considered rather on the prudish side. I never accepted any engagements in the Middle East, because there it's in your contract that you have to entertain the customers after you finish your act. And I would never have done that. To sit down with the men, and make small talk with them—that's not for me. I can't stand them. I really can't. Even simple invitations to go out to dinner, outside the cabaret, I never accepted; that even led to an argument with Josée.

. . . I had met Josée, who also did a two-girl dance number and wasn't getting along at all with her partner. We stayed together six and a half years, traveling all over the world. We were together on stage and off. That was really the life!

We had a lot of colorful adventures, things that happened that were amusing, some more so, some less. I could keep telling you about them for hours.

The most colorful? In Japan. Night spots there are huge. One we appeared in at Osaka, The Vale, was like going into a stadium: two twenty-four-piece bands, and two levels of tiered tables with over four hundred geishas!

The girls have a little radio receiver in their kimono

belts. Their boss, the "mama-san," sits at her switchboard, and when somebody asks for one of the girls as company, she calls her on this walkie-talkie setup. It gives a beep something like the tweet of a bird. So you get the strangest feeling when you walk in, as if you were inside a huge birdhouse . . .

Like all B-girls everywhere, the geishas do all they can to keep the customer interested in them while the show is going on. They don't want him to get so engrossed in it that he forgets what they're there for. But in Japan, the minute the act is over, the four hundred geishas would stand up like one samurai and go clap-clap with their little hands, without any expression on their faces, and then sit down again. It was really strange.

And the dressing rooms are really different from those in Europe. Very luxurious, with tatamis to rest on, a little heater to keep your teapot warm, and television.

In Israel there are some huge clubs, too, big enough to seat a thousand people. The Kaliph in Jaffa is an immense hangar of a place that is open on Sunday afternoons. People come in family groups, with the children. When the striptease numbers are coming on, the parents are warned, so the kids can be taken out into a side room where there is television to keep them entertained, as long as our G-string acts last.

But I never had any real hassles. People imagine all kinds of things about our profession. But it's no more dangerous to go around the world stripping than it is if you're selling Bibles or vacuum cleaners. White slavery and all that crap is just a lot of hogwash—or, if it does happen, it happens to tramps who'll sleep with anybody for dough, and that kind can get into just as much trouble turning tricks in the Bois de Boulogne.

I never hid from anyone what I was. Besides, all anybody had to do was see Josée and me live for a few days, and they'd have no more possible doubts. Not that we didn't know how to "behave," because I feel no need to provoke people or to shock them, but how can anybody fail to see it when two people are really "together"?

Of course, I didn't come into a nightclub and run up to the first guy I saw to grab him by his necktie and stare him down while I proclaimed, "I'm a lesbian, I love women, and you can go fuck off if you think you're gonna get me." But it wasn't long before they caught on, and then they laid off. Men aren't so stupid when it comes to that: They can pretty readily see whether you're only pretending not to be interested in them or whether you *really* have no use for them.

If they try to make a pass and get their noses twisted out of joint against an impenetrable barrier, even if it's invisible, they're not gonna try to bring the walls down, when they know there are so many other girls they can make out with.

In cabaret circles, we're not ostracized. All that may happen is that if we get too chummy with some gal, some of the well-intentioned tongues may whisper to her, "Watch your step! She's a dyke!"

But if she wants to risk catching our mange, she's free to try. Show people act like grown-ups.

Besides, for all practical purposes, every woman gives it a try, sooner or later—when you're on tour, or abroad, far away from your regular boyfriend, a little jaunt on the distaff side doesn't seem like any danger.

Gil had been great about our splitting up.

We were both sweet and tender little girls, not the kind to fight, or to make scenes, or to bear grudges. We had been wonderfully, madly in love with each other; she had been my first true love, and it was a marvel. But then I changed dancing partners. At first, I didn't like Josée. She was too sure of herself, more mature than Gil, much more positive. We hated each other, right off the bat . . . Then we rehearsed our act together, and the first night, after the show, she said to me, as naturally as could be:

"Coming home with me?"

And just as naturally, I told her, "I'll have to let Gil know about it first."

So I went home. I picked up a valise, and threw a few of my things into it.

"I'm going to live with Josée," I said to her.

She didn't protest, or shout, or yell. She was sitting on the edge of the bed, and just started crying without making any noise. I went over to her, and took her in my arms. I was crying, too. An unknown force was driving me toward Josée, but Gil—whom I no longer loved though I had not realized it until just now—was like my little sister and it hurt me to be hurting her. But what was out of the question, what I would not have put up with, was deception and lying. She had to go on living her life and I had to go on living mine.

With Josée, it just ended gradually, because that's the way life is. We felt the desire for each other less and less often, the lust was gone, but the main part remained: an infinite loving-kindness, the need to be in each other's arms when we slept, for instance.

We never, either of us, stayed out all night. We always came back home to crawl into each other's arms. It wasn't *sexual* anymore, but it was *sensual*. What we needed was to get back together, to feel each other's skin, her warmth, to kiss each other. She had a fling with one girl, and then it was my turn, I remember, at Modène on the Italian border, a gorgeous girl, a stripper who was the mistress of the owner of the cabaret we were appearing in. It was love at first sight: We wanted each other, and that very night. I went with her to her room, in the hotel above the club. We made love, magnificently. She was ardent, violent, passionate as only Italian women can be.

And then I wanted to get up, in order to go back to Josée.

"Stay with me," she urged. "I want us to spend the night together, so we can wake up together in the morning . . ."

"No, I just can't," I said. "My *amie* is waiting for me."

"You can't do that, really. Stay just a little longer."

I had gotten up. She was sitting on the edge of the bed, her legs spread. With her hands, she was spreading herself even wider open.

"Look," she said. "Look at me. Don't you like me? Don't you want to kiss me some more? To caress me? Come on, come back and lick me . . ."

Said that way, it may sound a little bit vulgar, but in Italian—that language is like a song—it wasn't quite the same thing. She was beautiful enough to kill, let alone eat, with red hair that came down to her shoulders, her head on the side, a long strand of hair hiding her eye that was still made up, a magnificent eye, black, with its false lashes, and a gaze that grabbed me. She was vamping me, making eyes at me, sinuous as a cat on the edge of the bed. She was really tempting, I tell you. I might almost have given in if I hadn't thought of Josée, who was up waiting for me.

"No, it's out of the question," I finally said. "I have to go back to my partner."

Then she became furiously angry. Raging like Vesuvius! Like Mount Etna! Like Monte Cassino!

"All you are is a lousy whore!" she yelled.

And, picking up the telephone, she screamed into it: "Doorman, when the signorina comes down, pay her off with a hundred thousand lire. And call a taxi for her, and pay her fare!"

I jumped on her, angry and furious. Who the hell did she think she was, anyway? We rolled down on the carpet, grabbed each other by the hair, like two panthers having at one another. Just picture it! Both of us in the buff, two strippers gone stark raving mad. Plenty of people would have paid to be able to see that tableau. And it was a real living one, believe me.

She had grabbed me by the throat and was trying to scratch me. She knew that was the kind of thing we can't put up with in the profession, scratches, black-and-blue marks, and the like. I fought back, rolling over on her. Then, straddling her, I shoved her shoulders down. She was quivering like an eel, and she was gorgeous, looking so mad, panting so, her belly vibrating between my thighs . . .

I slipped back a bit and, even as she kept fighting back just as hard, I saw the look in her eyes suddenly change. She let go of my neck, and her hands went to my breasts, with no intention of hurting them—heaven forbid! She continued to undulate beneath me, and I picked up the rhythm—and we made love again right there like two madwomen, violent but without any brutality, gone wild without any inhibition or modesty. A kind of war-for-the-fun-of-it, a real battle of the sexes. I fully understood the meaning of that expression there with her. When she got into the same position I had previously been in, I admired her body, erect above me, as I caressed her hips while she rubbed her cunt against me, her burning cunt that I could feel like a hot mouth on my thighs, my belly. What a beautiful bitch she was!

Her eyes half-closed, head thrown back, she was murmuring, *"Dio! Dio! Cristo! Che bella fica!"*

I didn't know too much Italian, but those words I could understand perfectly well: *"Dio! Cristo! Fica!"*

Two hours later, we had gotten back again to the same point as before, and I was asking, "May I leave now?"

We were both exhausted, tottering. She smiled, and replied in her singsong: "Now you can. At any rate, all your *amie* will have in her arms is a limp rag of a doll."

Even if I had confessed it to her, she never would have

believed that between Josée and me all that was left was great tenderness, but it was so very, very important.

But you're in a very dangerous situation when your heart is on one side and your desire is on the other. You risk coming across some new woman who may bring you both at once. That's what happened with Josée.

I split five years ago. We shared our savings equally, Josée and I; she took over the management of a restaurant, and I went and took courses for a year and then started this business, which is going along quite well. I can't complain; I have remained in the beauty business, and am surrounded by women. I never could have done anything but a job that brought me into contact with women all the time. And, besides, I like the fact that I help to make them beautiful.

As for the others, my fellow artistes, some of them are still around. There is no set retirement age in the stripping business. It all depends on how well preserved you are. I know one who is forty-one with a pair of breasts that would be the envy of most girls of twenty-five . . .

There are very few young ecdysiasts. The business is dying out. There is no one to carry on. Stripping has been killed by the live sex shows and hard-core porn.

It's true that my current girl friend is a little on the butch side. That's funny, because in the beginning, when I was very young, I only loved girls who were very feminine like me, my femmes, my mirrors, my sisters . . .

I guess it was with Josée that my taste in that changed, if one can put it that way, because with a lesbian, whether she be femme or not, she's still just a woman, and once she's naked in bed you're just two women who love and are loving each other. Josée, without question, "deformed" me, in the sense that she relieved me of all formalities, things to do, errands, and so on. She took charge of everything, carried the luggage, and all I had to do was follow behind with my Yorkshire terrier and my vanity case. It was taking the easy way, but how I loved it! I was the little thing you pet and protect. She did all that to perfection, and without crushing me in the process, without playing the tough guy, or the bulldyke. So I in turn became more feminine, whereas before her I was always the one who took the lead in everything and made the decisions.

What didn't change, either before or after her, is my total dislike for skirts! I feel totally ill at ease in a dress. I've never known how to walk in one. It's true, I could move much more easily dressed like Eve . . .

I could have gone on stripping onstage for a few more years, but I no longer felt like going off on tour for months and months and leaving her behind. Pascale, whom I had just met, represented stability to me, a quiet, solid, sure love. Even though she had been there and back.

Before me, she had never had an affair of any length. She was always on the prowl, here and there, just like a guy. Her technique? Plain and simple. She would drive up and say, "Can I drop you off someplace?" What went on inside her car would fill books!

Now the two of us live together just like the others around us, in the same settled bourgeois manner.

We have our flat, our TV, our little farm in Normandy. What else do people want? We are happy. I am happy.

Despite my profession, I was never one for living it up, or maybe just because of it. Knocking about from town to town, from cabaret to cabaret, I assiduously tried to maintain some equilibrium by living a quiet life.

I'm happy now, and completely so. My hunt for love, for understanding, for a shared life that would be both tender and merry, neither gray nor red but pink and blue, my exhausting march in the pursuit of happiness, has finally come to an end.

Is there a likelihood we may split up someday? Could be. Who can tell what will happen in the future? Only, with each passing year Pascale penetrates more deeply into my being. Each memory, each milestone, each shared event in our life binds me more closely to her, makes her more mine, as I become more hers.

Even our physical love, though it evolves and changes, has in no way lessened. Sometimes, on her skin, I can discover tastes that I never yet knew existed. Yes, perhaps with Pascale I have finally found happiness for a lifetime.

FRÉDÉRIQUE

What about the women who have made bad marriages, who are imprisoned, and who love women just as much as we virgins do, yet who could not or did not get going on time, which is to say, right from the start?

Those who married too early, because that was the thing to do, because they were ignorant, or weary, or discouraged, and then found themselves caught in a trap, in a maze without Ariadne's thread, my sisters who for the sake of their children remained in a household that meant nothing to them, stirring up cold ashes that had a bitter taste, and then because of those children who never asked to be born made the sacrifice of their loves, their pleasures, their entire lives.

Are they admirable women or are they just fools? Or could it be that they are both at once?

Bleeding, torn pelican-women,* one day those children to whom they devoted all of their love, to whom they dedicated their entire life, those peeping fledglings whom they protected with all of their warmth, will leave the nest and fly away to live lives of their own.

How much time will they have left then, to fulfill their own destiny, to take into their arms those women whom all through their years they have been yearning for, like the dazzling toys in a display window outside of their reach?

Are they really to be admired for having been faithful

---

* Common French symbol of total parental self-sacrifice, derived from Alfred de Musset's *La Nuit de mai*, as used in English in William Congreve's earlier "What, wouldst thou have me turn pelican, and feed thee out of my own vitals?" in *Love for Love*. (TR. NOTE)

to the "conjugal hearth" because they were afraid to go against conventions, didn't want to ruffle prejudices, were worried about what people would say?

Battered wives stay on in bondage because, having no profession, no way of making a decent living, with children to take care of, what else could they do? Take a tiny maid's room somewhere, go out to do housework, and turn their kids over to day-care? Only with an awful lot of courage, an awful lot of bruises, and a body beaten black and blue can they finally resign themselves to doing that.

Do they remain pinned down for the same reasons—with the same kind of bruises on their soul?

Are they to be pitied, or laughed at, or should we bow down before them—they who have never known the happiness of falling asleep and waking up in the arms of a woman they love, they who must always put on an act, ceaselessly pretend, laugh when they feel like crying, live with an identity which is not their own, hold their tongues, betray their real tastes, which are in no way shameful, and hide their mistresses, who will never be able to be their mates?

How can one judge? How can one know? . . . There they are, near us, and yet so far, with their dreams, silences, loves, and prisons.

* * *

August 12, 1977

Madame (or should I address you as "My dearest Elula," with respectful affection?):

. . . I worked up the nerve to read the proclamation of your faith, my own, all of ours, at one sitting, in one day, at the office, and it was a rare pleasure. I have come out of it with both a battered soul and a heart set free. I had been waiting for this forever, and it seems to me, with all due modesty, that I might have, should have, written it myself.

The endless scribblings that I treasure in my desk drawers at least bear witness that I tried . . .

But where can I turn when I am nothing but a humble secretary in a huge multinational armaments factory, bursting with important personalities, in which, out of deference to current demand, there's one female executive or engineer for every half a hundred males?

I won't be coming to your discotheque. That kind of place is more suited to beautiful, graceful women, to the sort of goatlike creatures I go hunting for myself whenever I am on the prowl, but whom I don't have the good fortune to be one of. To be a lesbian is a fact of life, a status, a race, a nationality. To be both a lesbian and homely is a curse. So I cruise on my own, a small, fortyish, graying she-wolf, voracious—but because of the scars left from two broken love affairs separated by thirteen years, I've locked my heart away.

Those are all the things, Elula, that I would have liked to be able to talk to you about. It happens that my family obligations (yes, I'm married, and have two children— where is the hiatus?) make it necessary for me to leave on vacation this very day. How I look forward to these three weeks: all those trailer camps and campsites can sometimes be full of delicious surprises! So I'm off on the prowl once again.

I leave it entirely up to you whether you wish to remain in touch with me, as it may suit your will and your fancy. Having said all this, you and your quiet courage and your wild moonshots leave me curious—not a curiosity motivated by sentimentality, but by confidence and tenderness.

Frédérique

September 9

Well, it's true then, isn't it, Elula? One can finally be heard if she yells loud enough, since you did answer my letter. I must admit that I have only the vaguest recollection of what I wrote in my emotional state (your book still burning in my mind), the way a person throws a bottle into the sea. I really don't know how to say thanks—maybe because I haven't had enough occasions in my life to be thankful for. Yet, I thank you for the kind of wild and raging joy which has brightened an otherwise unenthusiastic return from vacation.

What you tell me about the mail you have been receiving does not come as any surprise to me. I encounter in others that kind of distress and loneliness all the time, and often under the most respectable facades that can be. Women show an exemplary dignity in the ostracism that they suffer. But one doesn't have to listen too hard to hear all the howlings that are muzzled by what some jerks call Society, with a capital *S*, for Shittiness. And in calling these jerks *cons* as we do in French,* I'm quite aware that we are doing an injustice to that term—for, as some humorist has pointed out, they lack both its charm and its depth!

I described it as an unenthusiastic return from vacation, because it had nothing in store for me but the prospect of the eleven months that lie ahead before next year's summer vacation, eleven months to be spent in this office, looking across at the woman I love and who unfortunately no longer loves me. It's an unhappy spot to be in, for sure, but I have so far found no way to free myself from her. I'm no longer with her, but also am not without her. I don't know

---

* The French word *con* (cunt), used as both noun and adjective, denotes a stupid or silly person or thing; along with its derivative *connerie*, stupidity, it has passed today into the vernacular, almost totally losing its original anatomical overtones. Only in the most formal polite society does *con* still remain unacceptable, although it was once current only in the underworld and among the military, later gaining gradual respectability through its adoption by students, artists, bohemians of all sorts. (TR. NOTE)

of anything that's harder to bear. The situation actually drove me to suicide (failed, of course—but then, have I ever made a go of anything in my mess of an existence?). Now . . . It's really the pits. I have to cruise like crazy to try to get myself out of it. You see, she is worthy of my esteem, whatever she may have done, and so I keep flaunting my cruising to set her mind at ease.

Eight hours every day, I have to play the cock of the walk (if that expression can apply!). I make the most of every glance I've exchanged with any other woman, then kid aloud about all my "affairs," because I so enjoy hearing her laugh. And my evenings are devouring me with weariness and despair, but the main thing, at least for now, is to keep her from knowing it. For, while she may not love me anymore, she does like me very much (what a horrible thing!) and there is no reason for her to be hurt on my account, however much I may hurt over losing her. This may all seem confused, Elula, but you'll have to excuse me, because I still can't speak with detachment about our beautiful but lamentable love; after all, there are some dishes that become palatable only when they cool off!

I keep telling myself that I must never again let myself get locked into that golden circle of illusion, *le grand amour*. That's what I tell myself when I'm down at the trough of the wave, in a sunless place. After that . . . Well, I finally have to laugh, because I know what I'm like: Those great resolutions remind me of how it used to be every year at the beginning of the school term, how I carefully covered and labeled my textbooks, calligraphed the titles of courses on the outside of my notebooks, and studied so diligently for the first few weeks. Then, suddenly, in the dust of a sunbeam I would spot a drunken bee or a wild butterfly, and pfft! bye-bye, conscientious schoolgirl. I couldn't have cared less whether $a + b = c$. But if my cat surprised me with a new litter of kittens, or the edible mushrooms did not appear at the spot where I expected them, or unexpected tides swamped the local fishing fleet, I was moved to tears.

I'm making light of all this, but with the most tender irony. I know only too well that if, tomorrow, there was a chance to scamper after one of those goats, down a path where you get scratched to bits on the hawthorns, I'd rush in and get all bloodied without even trying to mark out my way. Maybe that's where my true sense of humor resides, in the fact that I know I'm still able to go and do mad things, despite all the slaps in the face and kicks in the ass.

It's funny—no, that's not the right word—it's strange. I observe things with amused interest (you become mistrustful when you live behind a mask) and I hate talking about myself. With you, I don't feel even that elementary distancing from myself that I generally practice, as if I had known you for eternity.

Friendship at first sight is something that I've experienced only once before, but I am nevertheless sure that it does exist. I have no idea when you and I may ever meet, as I can't get out very easily, being so fully occupied by my duties as a devoted-mother-who-does-everything-she-ought. We'll see; I'm not impatient about it. In fact, I have no real need of it, because I've always reveled in relationships by mail, perhaps because I feel much more comfortable in front of a blank page than when I'm face to face with someone I have everything to learn about. Am I shy? Of course.

If you feel an itch to write during the month of September, you can find me at my friend Simone's, because at that time Jacques will be away on his vacation. Simone—well, she's something. For fifteen years I've had an unbroken friendship with her. She's a Diana who goes out hunting men like some people hunt deer, an Amazon who, despite (or because of?) her wild pursuit of the male to be conquered, has been sniffing at my truffle all these years without knowing whether or not one day she'll decide to cross the Rubicon! I observe her hesitation waltzes with amusement and tenderness, and make no sound or sign. During last vacation, I spent one night under her seaside roof on the Île de Ré, which I so enjoy. A chaste night, but a hot one, oh, how hot!

You're in luck that my time has run out at the moment. I was on my way to writing one of those endless multi-volumed novels, and you would have had to put up with who knows how many more pages.

May I, Elula? I kiss you.

Frédérique

September 27

Greetings!

This fine fall weather puts vague yearnings in my soul and pins and needles in my heart. You give no sign of life, but no matter. I can imagine how busy you are, and am not impatient.

Notwithstanding the keen watch of Corinne, the terrible dragon who sits opposite me week after week, tender and completely un-understanding, curious and silent, reticent and assured, possessive while pretending indifference, I've discovered a new goat path! Is she beautiful? Better than that: alive! I've adored so many statues that her liveliness, her peering golden eyes, her gold dancing tresses, her light laughing voice, all plunge me into an enchanted state which is doubtless a bit sophomoric but takes me back a number of years. More of that later.

My new courtship doesn't leave me much free time. I will tell you whether October 2 next, the day I round forty, brings me something wonderful or turns out to be just a mirage. I extended my invitation, it was accepted; who am I to try to prejudge how it will turn out?

Yours, *Frédérique*

September 29

. . . My courtship was nothing but a prelude to a fine slip on the ice; in short, I fell flat on my ass. Well, such things do happen, and they leave my heart aching for a while, so don't hold it against me if I do a little groaning. If I can't complain to you, to whom can I?

Despite the apparent solidity, there's a woman underneath: Just peel away the surface . . .

I'm a good mother but am aware that I'm not giving my all. So I make up for it by devotion, tenderness, and imagination. As far as anyone can see, I'm just perfect, active, efficient, cultivated. But under the mask I'm dying.

There are off periods: the times when I follow women in supermarkets, when I gorge myself on a gesture or an attitude, the times when I am tempted by every kind of escape —alcohol, drugs, suicide.

I know I am an out-and-out lesbian and I feel no shame over that fact. What gets me down is that I have to pretend. The women I love think that I am taking charge of them, whereas in fact they give me the only strength I have. Then they go off, knowing that I am not free, and I encourage them to, hard as it is for me. I just can't be anybody's future . . . only their litmus paper.

My husband has guessed the truth and sometimes accepts it, though more often he turns it to his advantage; having caught on, I think, he wishes that he had "caught" me at it, like a little boy . . .

Clearly, I'm not very cheerful this morning!

But what is this I see? A café-au-lait smile, a burnt-toast complexion, the stride of an indolent queen—that's Marie-Jeanne, our girl of the islands, coming my way. My soul suddenly feels like that of a rum-drunk buccaneer and I have to go over and tease the wench a bit. She likes that.

I kiss your hands, and ship ahoy!

Frédérique

October 1

"Virtue, like the crow, nests in ruins." (Jules Renard)

Just received the wink from you that friend Simone passed along, Elula, and that lightens my downbeat morning a little.

Your family reunions make me drool with envy. I've just had a dose of my own, and my heart's plastered over with my petty bourgeois relatives: the sisters-in-law, and the brothers-in-law who are on a frighteningly familiar basis with the bottle (talk about letting oneself go!). And on top of that bunch a gang of shouting, fighting kids, all of them real little he-men, as their proud mommies keep asserting, as if that were something to gloat over. And it all takes place in a beautiful landscape in Anjou. The only advantage to this kind of an affair is that when I come back from one I always find an unexpected charm in my office and even enjoy smelling the polluted Parisian air . . .

It's a Monday like any other, Elula, with the usual schedule of meetings and other enjoyable exercises of that ilk. I have learned to sit for hours, my stoical fanny on some nameless chair, surrounded by the smoke and smell of the characters who are the top brass of my department—while constantly being watched out of the corner of her eye by a woman executive who keeps wondering whether I *am*, scratches her head to try to figure it out, knows nothing but guesses a lot, and might really be willing to give it a try—but then, that would be truly perverted! Well, seducing a woman who made her way up the ladder through the pants of some old fart in top management would strike me as being about as exciting as taking candy from a baby. Yech!

All this rambling on about my intrigues: I don't know how it strikes you; but I'll be back to you again soon. Kiss-kiss.

Frédérique

* * *

The next evening Frédérique came to see me; it was her birthday. She was just as she had described herself, just as I expected her to be. Not pretty, oh, no! tiny, petite, hair cut any which way, wearing thick glasses over mischievous eyes.

To celebrate being forty, Frédérique had decided to go all out. She wanted to round this bend, the way people used to cross the Equator, with great pomp and circumstance.

* * *

November 5

Elula mia,

Here I am in the office on a Saturday, a "catching-up day." And it's no fun. The boss has just been here pacing around the joint, bawling hell out of two or three of the younger people before turning on his heel and taking off. All things considered, I think I still prefer working with his assistant, bitch though she be.

A bitch, but a woman; I can always get around them, I know that type all too well. As for the other females in the department: There are two typists who have had all the life knocked out of them by unrewarding work and too many babies; one corresponding secretary who's kind of nice but whose main conversation is made up of the recipes in Tante Marie's cookbook; four rather overage file clerks, who are very dimly lit. And, since there has to be at least one miracle, Corinne—my wonderful dragon . . .

And as for me . . . I'm just a silly old sentimentalist, a softie and quick to empathize, infested with scruples (those "lice of the soul"), and infinitely respectful of others. Starved for affection: I have as much need to be loved as I have need to love. My childhood brought me all the delights reserved for "refugees"; my parents were in the Resistance, which left me full latitude to roam the countryside. I had no studies to speak of. Once I passed the required exams, I wanted to earn my own way, not to be dependent on anyone, and especially not on my mother, who, through her "perfection," was an unwitting castrator. I had two years of schooling in executive secretaryship and then right away a big adventure—off to the West Indies with a senator who was campaigning there. It was a dream job. I've never had a chance to go back to Guadeloupe since then, but it's always there, my green island (Karukéra, its earliest name, meant that), somewhere down in the most secret part of me. When I got back, there was Malika, who initiated me voluptuously . . . And since then—what a lot of foolish things I've done, like wanting to have a baby. I picked the father out with great care, as if one could find the best possible odds of heredity. He's intelligent, vulnerable, and handsome. His son is like him. I must say I'm proud of my elder son, because he's just as grand physically as he is mentally. He has the real innate elegance of old France and is reserved, modest, sensitive. He's thirteen, and makes noises about being a Beatles freak, but in his own room he listens to Mozart.

And then, while I was purring along waiting for my child to be born, I met up with a nice guy who wanted me and got his way by wearing me down, assisted by everyone in the family. It was a quick, quiet marriage, as if it was already clear that nothing good would ever come of it for me. A second child was born, but seven years later. And then came the downfall of our household, which is now nothing more than the unsuccessful coupling of two lonely, separate people—something my husband is not ready to admit.

My younger son is very much like me, fanciful, unpredictable, irresistibly appealing but inclined to get into all sorts of trouble; he's always on the lookout for the window to break, but equally on the lookout for the big kiss that'll make it all all right.

There's little to add to that picture. I like Mozart, Barbra, Beethoven, Charles Morgan, Baudelaire, Paul Éluard, Picasso, Manet, the *Nouvel Observateur*, beans *à la charentaise*, coffee, dark tobacco, vodka, Elula Perrin, Bach, Schubert, Souchon, Marilyn Monroe, my beautiful cat, the rain on the cliffs of my hometown and the sun everywhere else, storms, Breffort, new Beaujolais, light simple furniture, the Bible, Simone, my nostalgic memories of Malika, my work, my escapes into letter writing, *The Lacemaker* . . . All of that pell-mell, and in no order of preference. I like anything that's alive, that suffers, that cries when it's hurt. I think (but I'm only whispering this to you) that I love life, in all of its forms and in spite of its lousy tricks!

Well, that's a fairly chaotic portrait, but honest! Oh, yes, what I love above all is sincerity; I can't stand lies.

I leave you to your life, Elula, as I slip out on tiptoe. Tonight I'm going to concentrate again on my exacting but enriching technical translations: It's wonderful to know that just through the grace of your style you can make wave guides sing and radars dance.

I kiss you.

Frédérique

November 17

Penelope is back! For months, we've had a little spider in our office. Ever since the big October cleaning, we haven't seen a web, and we thought those monsters had done her in. But what a miracle! In the sunlight, I just saw some threads shining, between the telephone stand and the lamp. So, Penelope is there in her corner. One of these days, she'll light on my typewriter. She wanders onto it with tiny steps, and then stops on the cover, probably because it's warm there . . .

Strange thing, Elula, we don't see the world in the same way, you and I: You are just going to bed when I get up, and you get up when I turn in!

Frédérique

You asked me what I meant by "the main artery." That's the nerve center of our whole company. It's where you find the mail service as well as the infirmary, the building administration office as well as the cafeteria, the coffee and croissant machines, the big conference rooms . . . It's Montparnasse at rush hour. Mostly you see all the people there who have a little time on their hands and go wandering about, hands in their pockets, listening for the latest gossip. That's the place where new flirtations start and old affairs get broken off.

One should never go unannounced into the cloakrooms or the toilets, because there are unspeakable things taking place there! All the other corridors look like passageways, with rows of identical doors and unbroken straight walls. The main artery *lives*, there's no work done there, or only very rarely. In a word, it's the playground for recess. And it's also my flower market: child-women, blossoming women, women-women. That's where I meet the Hélènes, the Christines, and the others. That's where you can send each other looks so eloquent that they're as good as dates. It's my own hunting preserve!

OK, then, so much for this week, otherwise I'll miss the mail clerk. Farewell, my regal one, and see you soon. I respectfully kiss your aristocratic paw.

Frédérique

November 18

I like the voices of the women who answer the phone for you. They sound like you. Today was a day for the commissary and the discotheque—all because of Sylvie. As in the case of the main artery, the discotheque is more a meeting place than a music room. We go there to borrow records, but mainly to rendezvous on the benches and whisper confidences to each other that are nobody else's business.

And besides, Sylvie is so pretty! It's strange how long it always takes me to fill out my forms when I'm doing it over at her desk. I sometimes wonder why I ever let those deliriously blue eyes, those dimples, that soft skillful mouth get away. She was just a passing fancy. But I guess she still turns me on—because my darling dragon claims that Sylvie gives me "the itch" and that I eat her so with my eyes that one of these days I'm going to hop on top of her right in the middle of the discotheque.

Anyway, as if by pure chance, Irene and Danièle and Josyane were there, as well as some little thing I had never seen before who was very obviously cruising Josyane. I wish her a lot of pleasure (which she'll get!) as well as plenty of courage if she's going after that iceberg. When I tried, it took me over a year, and then with the sudden decision of the shy, I asked whether she'd have lunch with me, laughing loudly all the time, and miraculously the goddess deigned to accept. After that, as we went on from the *crudités* to the sweetbreads in Madeira sauce . . .

But really, you shouldn't think that I spend forty-one hours a week at my factory doing nothing but seeing how I can make out. I work there, too, you know, and hard as can be. Only, like all well-organized lazy people, I get my work out of the way in a hurry, in order to have some time to myself. Then when I can't face any more paper work, I get up and walk around—rarely by myself, that's the point.

About women, I have an entomologist's curiosity; they fascinate me, and my interest in them is not always (far from it) visceral in nature. I listen to them. It's very hard to get them to talk about themselves, but once you get the engine going, they take off like the Concorde.

We bounced around like Ping-Pong balls in the company bus last night, the bus that drops us all off at the various gates of Paris and then picks us up again the next morning, while we're all still loused up with sleep, coffee, and the kids who were late for school.

But I wonder what ever got into me that made me drop my little goat and go wallow in Françoise's bright eyes. I must really be nostalgic, and it makes me either cry or die with laughter! To think that those two, both of whom are infinitely better than I, and certainly a lot more attractive, should fight like cats and dogs all on account of me . . . I rub my chin thoughtfully, and don't understand how it can be . . . Not trying to understand is the first step of wisdom. No matter how much I look into my mirror (mirror, mirror on the wall, am I still the silliest one of all?), I can't find any answer there that satisfies me. So, is it all in the head—and the hands?

For a very long time I was inhibited by my homeliness.

That complex was dispelled in part by Malika and then by the cruising I got thrown into by our breakup, and all the despair that that caused me had no other purpose than to prove something to me about myself. What is beauty, Elula? I believe that there's only one door it can open: the one to a man's bedroom.

You may take that opinion to be somewhat—yes, somewhat scornful. I feel that I am completely torn, at once naïve and blasé, ready to hope for anything and to renounce anything. For the past two years I have been on the defensive; I attack before I get bitten myself, and yet each new encounter finds me blocked with apprehension. I guess I'll remain a virgin all my life!

So, fuck Vauban and military engineering, my superb one, I'm off to make the rounds of the main artery. I kiss you,

Frédérique

* * *

Frédérique came back to see me again. She was dead drunk. One of those flowers that she admires while also gathering honey from it, one of those paths down which she loves to stray, had just died at Bicêtre Hospital from a galloping cancer.

She was a mess, weaving, hiccuping, tinier than ever, her three stray gray hairs standing on end on her little sparrow's head, her face twitching wildly while she cursed both gods and men through tight lips. I had to forbid her to have anything more to drink.

"Have that fuckin' music shut off!" she mumbled.

"Look, this is a nightclub, not a cemetery."

I was deliberately rude to her, the way you slap a person who is about to faint. I had to snap her out of her fog, save the little dinghy from the storm. And a discotheque is hardly the ideal place for the first howls of a broken heart. It's a place to come to later on, to get drunk on sound and movement when the wound has begun to heal already. That evening I had to carry the rebellious, babbling little rag doll out to a taxi.

* * *

November 20

"I recognized happiness by the noise it made as it left."

Well, yes, Elula, I'm getting over it. You have to come out of the worst shitholes as quickly as possible so as not to let them kill you . . . And besides, the hyenas are standing by, licking their chops, watching my reactions, setting traps, trying to get my attention or my pity . . .

At home, everything has gone to hell. My night on the town decided the man to call in the whole family. One after the other, I had to put up with mother, sister, and aunt. But I finally sent them all packing, in no uncertain terms. They really piss me off, Elula. All of them drive me to my wits' end and then want to have me sent to a rest home. So that, later on, in case of a divorce, they can establish that I am not competent to take proper care of my children. And the fight I put up is only for the kids. So I have to build up a record, in order to be able to defend myself.

Several of the people who live in my tower are ready to sign affidavits for me. To my great amazement, I've been finding a degree of friendliness and warmth in housewives who I thought didn't know any world existed outside their three-room flats.

More soon,

Frédérique

December 8

Corinne is surely right these days when she claims I'm as eager for a good lay as a horny rabbit. These first signs of winter make women look so beautiful that I feel I've become all eyes. What a fabulous sight there was to see this morning when I got on that bus! A cameo of an Anna (dark hair, green eyes). A blue-and-gold Sylvie all dressed in black, gazing deliberately, expressionlessly at a Colette in a long green coat . . . And then, once I was in my dear main artery, a dazzling Josyane with her white smile and lightly touching voice, an admirable Huguette . . . By all the saints, they're gonna drive me nuts, those devil-sent creatures! I feel all full of sunshine on account of them, for all this rotten weather we're having, so long as my head keeps cool.

One thing is sure, winter has favored me this year. And do you know that you've had a lot to do with it? After all, Elula, what was getting me down was my loneliness. Not having anyone to talk to. Because, while I listen a lot, I don't say anything, or very little indeed. It seems to me that what really needs to be said can't be—except to you, because you can represent what we obscure ones, we rank-and-filers, have to keep hidden. That last little bit that we must hide makes an enormous difference.

I dream of sincerity and authenticity. That last word scares me because it's been so distorted with overuse, but, given its real meaning, you'll agree that it would sometimes be wonderful to be able to be authentic. I feel most of the time like I'm wearing a disguise—the disguise of an oh-so-respectable lady, of a respectable mother, respectable wife, respectable secretary, a respectable blah. So the only respect I have is the respect I feel for others.

But then, I'm not being fair, you're not the only one I can talk to. There *is* Corinne. My fine dragon and I are on our way toward what may turn out to be a very real friendship. I don't know who it was who said that the only difference between love and friendship is the width of the bed. In our case, that's absolutely true. Since desire has disappeared, our feelings have grown more expansive. I feel more at ease with her. I can say anything I want to her, and share the splendor of a barely opened rose, the song of a little sparrow at the window, the strange resonance of a poem, the difficulties of a hard crossword puzzle. Everything and nothing or, in other words, all that counts. Whether she's aware of it or not, she's indispensable to me. I have to breathe her oxygen, because my own isn't enough for me. I guess the two years of daily crucifixion to reach this point were well worth it, don't you? I have no regrets at all, on her account. In fact, I've been almost wondrously surprised to realize that I have few regrets about anything. I haven't done much harm in my life. Remorse? Never heard of it. Mistakes? I'm paying for them.

In four and a half years, my elder son will reach his majority, and without looking back I'll depart the conjugal hearth with my younger one in tow. What then? Well, then, as my dear old granny used to say, "It'll be no worse than the good Lord wishes."

But what do I see? Indeed, there is Queen Josyane, under full sail, heading across the parking lot toward my office. Heavens!

Well, here I am back again! Ladies' imaginations know no limits and Josyane had an ironclad alibi to justify her

Frédérique

unexpected call on me: She needed the blueprint of a radar that was produced within my department. Nevertheless, I pointed out to her, when she left with the print rolled up under her arm and spouting all kinds of totally useless mumbo jumbo, that the blueprint was probably available on every desk on her floor—after all, it had been turned out for the use of her department! These lightning meetings remind me of boarding school, and the dates the girls made to meet in the shadowiest depths of the dormitories. At that time, I couldn't have been less interested, because I still thought there was more fun to be had with lads of my age. In fact, my vacation in England had rather turned my stomach, because the little English girls made no secrets of it: They walked about with their arms around each other, kissed each other at the movies . . . French girls were much more decorous as I saw it. Now I just think, more hypocritical. I can assure you that I'd get a perverse kick out of seeing those Sheilas and Shirleys again, and especially that Eileen, who shed so many tears over me, as I now realize!

Hoping to hear from you soon.

Frédérique

December 19

Since knowing you, I like people a little more and my cat a little less.

. . . The hours here have been so tightly strung together. I don't even have any time to kill; time is more likely to get the best of me. Year's end, in places like the one I work in, is sheer madness. You'd think we were busy giving Christmas presents to African kings and other oil potentates, the feverish, speedy way deals get thrown together. So there's a lot of work to be turned out by the five old machines in the department, including my own.

I often wonder what kind of a poet dreams up the names they use for the complicated hardware we create in this place. Symphony, Canopus, Aladdin, Aquitania, Cerberus, Centaur . . . And then the awful ones: Cactus, Cobra, Rattler, Javelin . . . And the sweet ones: Éliane, Esmeralda. One I specially like is Felix, but that's only because it reminds me of one of my friends' cats.

Corinne asked me a question yesterday that I didn't know the answer to: "What's your sign? I know you were born in March, but are you Pisces or Aries?"

Do you have any faith in astrology? I do. Malika once cast my horoscope for me, but I lost it at some point during one of my eighteen later moves. It's strange to note that all of those various peregrinations remain very vivid in my memory and that their clearest reference points are women's faces. Whatever became of Perdida-Cité Universitaire, Elisabeth-Paris XIII, or Mado-Paris XV? But there's a clear sequence from Marie-Bagneux to Manuelle-Montparnasse, Paola-Clamart, Arlette-Sceaux, Andrée-Fontenay Number Two (Fontenay Number One was Malika herself), Colette-Saintes, Ginette-La Rochelle, Souris-Antony, etc. . . . Not to mention Châtillon—I'm not giving you a full report on my hunts . . .

Aha (very theatrically, if you please)! It looks like Sylvie is heading my way. See you later, if it turns out that way; this is a chance that's not to be missed, even out of friendship.

OK. It *did* turn out. Suddenly, there I was, without knowing too well how I got there, in a delightful apartment right on the edge of the Clamart forest. I've come back from it with my head and my heart filled with shooting stars. And since it's four in the afternoon already, it seems supererogatory to me to try to do any more work.

Sweet Jesus! (This reminds me of the sweet time when

Corinne and I used to dash out of here several times a week at unusual hours, and, as if to be less conspicuous, even had the gatekeeper order us a taxi. I guess I don't have to worry about spoiling my reputation anymore at this point!)

I think it's very praiseworthy of me to have come back to this letter after that session at Clamart! I'm sure men, with their usual eloquence, would call my Sylvie a "ball-drainer," and that's just about what it amounts to.

I don't know whether I'll get a chance to write you again before the end of this blasted year. So, what should I wish you?

Pell-mell, here's a whole trunk full of wishes; choose among them, and keep what you like best . . .

Frédérique

* * *

Frédérique and I had lunch together early that January.

I was beginning to know pretty well what my Frédérique is like, with her terse, concise style full of poetry and humor. Yet, there we sat across a table, staring at each other over a couple of *croque-monsieur* (of all things);* although we'd gotten together to talk about women, we weren't too sure just what to say to each other. There was deep complicity, deep empathy between us; but, as she said so well in the second letter she wrote me, our "physical" meeting didn't add much to the pleasure we had both gotten from our correspondence.

What advantage was there to it? The warmth of eyes meeting, and a chance for me to talk to her, since I write her so little and phone her so rarely.

She knows practically all there is to know about me,

---

* Literally, "gobble-mister," the quaint French name for a ham-and-melted-cheese sandwich. (TR. NOTE) having read my book before meeting me. I'm the one who has to ask her questions so as to shed some light on the areas that the jigsaw of her letters, whether deliberately or not, had left unfinished.

She tells me just what she feels like telling, but I've no way to make her go any further. That untamed modesty of hers . . .

"I've really only been in love with two women," she says, "Malika and Corinne."

"But what about all the others?"

"The others? Just ports in the storm. My life is a trail of trees of all varieties. I blazed each one with a little touch of feeling, but never with a piece of my heart. Twice scalded, with thirteen years between—that's enough for me."

"Why are you waiting for your older boy to come of age before you leave? What about the second one? Haven't you just set yourself that time limit out of cowardice? So as to push the horizon back, to delay the due date when you *have* to leave?"

"No, actually, it was my lawyer who advised me to wait until I had only one minor child. It's too long to explain to you, but he says it'll be easier for me to get custody that way."

"And what about your husband?" I want to know. "Will he let you go?"

"He'll pretty well have to. In spite of the fact that I'm pint-sized, the day I decide to leave, nothing, and especially not him, will be able to hold me back. You know, I'm familiar with his reactions. Men are made on a certain number of stereotyped models. You can almost always fit them into a category, and consequently, since they're preprogrammed, you can predict what they'll do without trouble. But try predicting the reactions of a woman! Or her whims! I can read my husband like an open book. But what the heck, in the final analysis, he's not a bad guy, things could have been a lot worse."

* * *

January 13

... I've told myself the whole story of Malika, so now I can tell you about her. It's a Penelope task, a hundred times taken up and a hundred times thrust aside out of discouragement, out of continual fear of betraying her, of not being up to portraying her correctly and paying her the tribute she deserves.

Our breakup? A catastrophe. When I was with her, I changed from head to foot; she brought about my rebirth. I believed in happiness, and made it the watermark of her life. When I found myself alone again, I panicked; and then, two years later, I made that decision to have a baby, with the crazy consequences that you know.

I've already told you, I don't really want to see her again, Malika, my bewitchment. I have such a dazzling memory of her that I don't ever want to test it against a reality that might prove disappointing.

And besides, how can you tell whether the people you've loved grow old gracefully, meaning not at all? I loved her too deeply to run any risks. "I loved her too deeply," in fact, doesn't really say it: I love her, and I guess I'll never love anyone but her. She is still always and forever with me, even though our breakup will have its sixteenth anniversary next June 9. That's what Malika was, an island in time: December 9, 1960–June 9, 1962.

All my restless cruising was really only a stopgap between two authentic passions. Between Malika and Corinne, there were ten pitiful years. How much time will there be between Corinne and X?

And since I'm telling you about my loves (the real ones, the only ones), how about my telling you about my brother? I was five years old when my parents started to get involved in the Resistance, seven when my father got himself arrested and shipped off to the concentration camp.

My confidant, my idol, my accomplice all that time was Pierre. He was in on all my first times, all my foul-ups, all those childhood joys that you never forget. I used to cry on his shoulder, when I hurt and when I was happy. Now we don't even have to say anything to each other anymore: We understand in silence. We have absolute harmony. Is there something Freudian in that? Could be, but if so it makes no earthly difference to me. Our relationship has been a full success and I'm not going to spoil it by looking for worms in a perfect apple; I'll take it just as it is.

I can remember well when I brought Malika home for a visit, back in the summer of '61. Brought face to face with the obvious, my mother decided to play the ostrich about it and hide her head in the sand.

But one evening she did make some snotty remark to me, and Pierrot, without even looking up from his dinner plate, said in his big gruff voice: "What's the matter, did the kid do something wrong? She didn't piss on your geraniums, did she? So how about laying off her, huh?"

That became a password between us . . .

It's true, what I told you about my children. The very idea of having a daughter filled me with terror. And you know, in the final analysis, you're just like me: For an adolescent girl you'd have been a jealous, tyrannical mother, I'm sure of it.

My boys don't bother me. They're not a part of me, and there's no umbilical cord to threaten them.

Oh, but if I'd had a daughter! . . . I can see just how it would be, I'd be suspicious, spying on her comings and goings, watching who she went with, worried over who would be her first guy! Yuch! All things considered, it's better that I had sons, even if, sometimes, I do feel I'm hopelessly alone.

I have the feeling that I've never told you this much about myself. Word of honor, I'm letting myself go. Do you mind, Elula? I'd better go make a trip down the main artery.

And here I am back again. No Josyane on hand at the discotheque, seems Madame is home with the flu. So there was no point in staying there. Sylvie, gorgeous as ever, greeted me with a very formal "Bonjour, madame," that knocked me on my can! How hypocritical can my divine ones be? I mean, that afternoon at Clamart wasn't so long ago!

Well, now, I really do have to be going. I don't want to. I feel like I could have gone on writing you all day long. I've no idea how much this letter will weigh and I hope you won't have to pay postage due on it, that would really top everything! . . .

Frédérique

VANINA

May I have your attention? On French television, there is an open-ended, talky program called "A Minute for Women." So if you don't mind, Society, would you let us have just "A Second for Lesbians"?

I don't think the story I have to tell is going to change any set opinions or preconceived ideas. It is just one more story, one more garland around the slim, frail neck of Woman, which is what we are. Me and all the others, those who were so long known as the cursèd or damned women, when all they really were was condemned.

What was it that damned them? Their forbidden loves? Judeo-Christian civilization, what a vocabulary of tears and blood you introduced into our lives! Thunderbolts and lashes, disciplines and penances, mortifications and remorse. And you call yourself the religion of Hope . . . Don't make me laugh.

I'm a Corsican, born of Corsican parents, an islander from the Mediterranean, where a woman walks on foot several paces behind her lord. I come from those Latin shores where women have been valued at less than nothing. There was nothing there to predestine me to such "cursèdness." Or to my profession, which is that of physician. Or indeed to my role in the feminist struggle. But you'll let me have my second to tell you all of that, won't you?

My parents were very poor people. In fact, even poorer than that. All there was in our house was a table, some benches, and some mattresses on the floor. My father did nothing: He was a fisherman. Not a professional fisherman, with a boat, and nets, and income—no, nothing like that, but just what he called "a private fisherman," which means, when the fancy took him, he went fishing, and when he came back he traded his catch for a few rounds of drinks in the bars of the port. He wasn't really a bad man; more likely he was a schizoid. The only times he even broke his stolid silence were when he resorted to violence. In those fits of fury, he would smash the table. Then he had to repair it so he could break it again the next time. That was the reason my mother never wanted to get any more furniture. What for? He'd only have smashed it all.

As a way of protecting ourselves from his fits, we took refuge in joy. All five of us: Mother, my two brothers, and my sister, Laetitia. We used to laugh all the time, over anything or nothing, bound together in this salutary conspiracy.

One night we laughed out of turn. On the table, there was a pot of bean soup with some fatback floating around in it. Father swept it all away, soup, kerosene lamp, and all—and naturally, he smashed the table.

So we went to bed without any dinner.

Laughter was our daily bread, our way of outwitting our misery, and also our way of outwitting adults, too: In front of other people, we always laughed, pretended to be doing it proudly, living our good life.

I don't know what it is to get angry. Scornful silence is the most violent form of refusal I ever display. If I got angry I'd be imitating my father; whereas Mother, abundant and destructive as Nature itself, was always in league with her children, so proud of their success . . . My mother was so near to us; we could huddle against her like crowding little sheep, dark of eye, wild, and forbidden to baa . . .

I think I began to steal as soon as I was able to walk. My very first step was taken in order to be able to reach something that didn't belong to me. I stole fruit, vegetables, poultry.

I remember when the first five-and-ten-cent store in Ajaccio opened on Cours Napoléon. That was one of my great hunting grounds. At the end of the first week of operations, it was six million francs in the red! Our whole school had gone there to lend a hand to the rest of the population.

I learned to read fairly late. I was six then. In our little village school, there was just one class. So I stayed on in its higher half, or second grade, for five years. I was a good student, headstrong, stubborn, eager to learn, but not open to any correction or adverse comment about the work I did. If any was voiced, I would take off into the maquis. Our village was set upon a high promontory that had all kinds of caves in it, and I'd run off there and stay for entire days.

The curriculum for the upper half of our single grade wasn't all that interesting, and I was beginning to know it by heart. At fifteen, I took the *certificat d'études* and passed it with the highest grade in the whole district, just as if I'd been through a regular grammar school.

My father had died in May, and I got my diploma in June. Two breaks for me in successive months: I was really in luck.

Armed with my previous diploma, after working on a farm for a year in order to save up a little nest egg, I went off to town. I got to Porto-Vecchio, found a dark basement without running water or electricity that I could rent cheap, crammed algebra all summer, and in October I was ready to enroll in the fourth form [ninth grade] at a lycée. The first three months I was thirteenth in the class, but by the end of the second trimester I was first. The next year, I was able to take the BEPC and got first place in all of Corsica.* That meant a scholarship, and a chance to go to Ajaccio and prepare for the *baccalauréat*.†

My little sister, Laetitia, was following me in schoolwork, just two years behind. I had taught her to read and write during all that spare time I had in the "second" grade. And one fine day we both had our *baccalauréat* degrees at last. We had worked hard for them and, I think, truly deserved them. What strenuous application, what stubborn obstinacy it demanded of the two of us—two little Corsican peasant girls, who, according to the fate that was all laid out for them, should very rapidly have become two of those silhouettes in black that guard the herds of goats and children in our stony, silent villages. But in Laetitia, as in me, there had been that strong desire and determination to get beyond ourselves.

Now we were ready to go and try our wings on the Continent, in Marseilles, where we landed with two cardboard valises full of figatelli, sausages, and dried beans enough to last us a full quarter of the year.

Through the classified ads, I had found myself a spot as a monitor at the Lycée of Sisteron. Three times a week I went into Marseilles by train, to attend laboratory classes. Laetitia went to live in a girls' hostel where room and board were cheap enough so I could help her meet it. She was starting out for her degree in mathematics, while I was doing my pre-med.

It's obvious I hadn't selected the shortest major to get a degree in, so I had no right to complain about the dire poverty I was going to have to put up with for those years.

Just a minute! Who said I was complaining?

There was still joy, still laughter. That great refuge of

---

* The BEPC, or *brevet d'études du premier cycle de second degré*, is the rough equivalent to completion of two years of high school. (TR. NOTE)

† Approximately a junior-college (A.A.) degree in the United States. (TR. NOTE)

laughter that, when we were children, had preserved us and bound us to our mother when the paternal squalls were unleashed, still stood us in good stead. I carried it with me as a snail carries its shell.

After I finished pre-med, I had to move to Marseilles proper. Through a university chum, I found what to me was a gold mine: a job as night clerk and watchwoman in a hot-sheets hotel in Rue des Feuillants; there was a closet under the stairway that had been furnished as a "studio," meaning that I could sleep there and do my work at a small desk, provided I never tried to stand up once I was inside the door.

That was where I spent my nights. I can still see myself there, nodding over an anatomy chart; at my right hand, a pile of fresh towels and condoms that went with the room key. The whores were darling to me. When the trick paid for the room, they'd exclaim in their southern accents, "Go on, throw in a little something extra for the coed, fuh goodness' sakes!"

Once I was in my second year, I was able to get some work as a night nurse. It didn't pay any better than the whorehouse in Rue des Feuillants had, but let's say it was at least a little more in keeping with my abilities and more useful for the profession I was heading toward . . .

To eke out my budget, on Saturday nights I sang at a Corsican cabaret. Laetitia accompanied me on the guitar. We were now living together again, having taken a small room near the Prado. The last two years, when we had seen each other only during vacations, had been hard on both of us. We were so close to one another, so "twinny," so tied to our mother in our blood and our flesh, that it was actually painful for us to be separated. Now we had something of a home again, and a group of friends, including you, Elula. You didn't have so much money either, out of your schoolteacher's salary, yet how many times you helped

Vanina

me meet my tuition fees at the medical school, or brought along food enough for a couple of days.

Do you remember the time you had been out fishing on your old pal Nicky's boat and, having had wonderful luck, brought me back a huge bag of fish? We weren't in, so you threw the package through a broken pane in one of our windows, on the ground floor—and when we got back, three days later, the whole building reeked hopelessly of your bountiful catch . . .

So here I am now in Paris, a gynecologist, doing very well, thank you, and a lesbian.

I'm a physician (another one of those words that in French we have no feminine for: There's ogress, and priestess, and even, if you must, doctoress—but no physicianess . . .).

So, as I said, I'm a gynecologist, but I have no intention of discussing homosexuality as a practitioner. Only as myself, Vanina, a woman among women, a lover among mistresses.

I am fully aware of the analytical schema that old Papa Freud might draw up to trace my beginnings and portend my ends. When I could at last dedicate myself to femininity, I wasn't about to find any answer in Freud, who had written of women as that unknown dark continent that would remain so until scientific developments taught us more about them . . .

But I am not speaking here as one of a group of specialists whose main interest lies in dissecting the ovary and studying a cross section of the heart that beats only for women. I am writing as my thoughts and my passions, my memories and my irritations move me to. A Danish poet(?) compared the orgasm to a sneeze. Truly poetic, indeed! Perhaps that is the way man experiences his own climax: ejaculation as explosion, the eruption of a volcano, an overflowing of lava, a popping champagne cork that lets the pent-up foam escape at last.

For woman, climax is an ocean swell, a tempestuous sea that rolls us, enfolds us, swallows us up, and drowns us. It's the suffocation of the mermaid out of water, the gasping for air, the mad skipping of the heartbeat, the hollowing of the gut, a gigantic tidal wave driving its wild undulations into the deepest of inlets.

Our climax is not an aggression. It doesn't explode; it implodes.

No geysers for us, but underwater swirls; no glue on the sheets, but the dewy traces that a snail at morning leaves on the frost.

That's what a woman's climax is like, Dansk poet—and Gesundheit! Sneeze all you like—without us.

My first orgasm . . . How to be specific about when it took place? I became conscious of my clitoris very early, because, wanting to imitate the boys (penis envy?), I peed standing up, pressing a reed against my clit to try to bring out an even stream.

My first—Juliet—was fourteen years old, and I was only nine. She lived on a farm up a bit from ours. I used to see her on Thursdays, when I was not out running through the maquis with my brothers, galloping like skittish goats, in the games that all the other boys in the village played. In fact, very often I was the leader. I could punch hard, just the way they did, and didn't have to worry so much about being kicked in the crotch. I made fun of their thingamajigs, that stupid, limp excrescence of flesh. It never would have occurred to me to want to feel it, whereas I adored petting the bird's down that covered my tender Juliet's mound.

Oh, we were hardly flaming woman-lovers! But neither were we indulging in the kind of games the little Sicilian peasant boys played in *Padre Padrone*, buggering the barnyard fowls, who didn't know what was happening to them.

No. Ours was joy as well as sport.

We would walk out together, go running hand in hand, laughing whenever we tripped, as we fell to the ground. The stones beneath our feet would roll away under bushes, and we rolled on the dry, mossless ground, among the wild rosemary and myrtle. We kissed each other on the cheeks as well as on the lips, and I kissed her on the little breasts she already had. Our fingers trembled more than they caressed; they gave us delicious thrills that ran over my skin and raised the grain on it the way cold weather does.

In that hot crackling grass, I'm not sure we ever even moaned. I can't remember. But I don't think so. We must have breathed a little bit faster, and then started to laugh nervously, and finally gotten up, shaking the dust out of our clothes as we started off to run elsewhere for further sport.

It was in Ajaccio that I met Vanina—Vanina, whose name was the same as my own, and who was so much like me.

But where I was tomboyish and exuberant, she was deeply solitary and shy.

I noticed her in the schoolyard, where we used to go after the refectory. She was a boarding student, whereas I slept at my own place. She would go off and sit by herself, reading, dreaming, looking into space. And for the first time in my life I found myself *looking at* another being. I would look at her, watch her living, try to memorize her slightest gestures, her least movements, spy on her while she was still totally unaware of my existence. I would look at her hands. Hands are so important. They are tenderness, they are creation, they are the things that strike and the things that help.

It went on that way all through the quarter. I started

hoping for the moments when I'd be able to watch her, impatiently awaiting the bells that punctuated our lives and ran our hearts.

We were eighteen.

In order to be able to see each other alone, since we weren't in the same class, we would make dates to meet in the rest rooms during classes. The boarding proctoress had a penchant for women, and especially for Vanina. The day she caught us hand in hand, while we were supposed to be there peeing, she put me on report, but not her.

That was the only time in my life that I failed to protest against an injustice, although you know I am ready to hop up on any barricade when justice or freedom is under attack. I was even happy over this particular injustice, for it spared the woman that I loved.

At Easter vacation, Vanina invited me to visit at her parents' house. We shared the same room, the same bed, and then shared our kisses, our caresses.

Vanina found it hard to accept the fact that she loved a girl and was loved by one in turn.

Yet she no longer existed without me, nor did I exist without her. She had long since understood the nature of the excitement she felt about me.

A year after we met, she went home to spend Christmas with her family and was to come and stay with me for New Year's.

She didn't show up, so I phoned.

Vanina had been run over by a car on her way to the railroad station.

She was twenty . . .

But life went on. I'm not one of those Corsican mourners. I'm not the kind to kill myself or to douse my head with ashes as I keen over the irreparable.

I continued with my studies: pre-med, med school, internship, gold medal for residency, specialization, first in my class, always and in everything.

I didn't want to become a part of a hospital: heading a clinic, teaching newcomers, becoming a professor. How could I, as a woman and a lesbian? Those were two capital-*O* obstacles. Did I ever feel the discrimination, the latent hostility, even when it didn't come to the surface! Once, before I had to take an oral examination, my mentor told me:

"Remember, you're not appearing *before* a board, you're going up *against* one . . ."

So don't let anyone tell me that such conditions don't exist, that it's all merit, and hard work, and the rest of that crap.

There are some women doctors who head clinics, just as there are some women chiefs of police, or airplane pilots, or ships' captains. But not enough to bother with. Just tokens to be used as evidence by the men in power. "*Sexist*, indeed! Why, look at Mrs. Whoozis, and Miss Whatsername!" (They don't even say Ms.) You know how it is, we all have to salve our consciences!

And are those ladies brilliant stars? More likely just meteors, quick to be booted out, finding a banana peel in every pair of rubber gloves, and orange skins on the gas levers!

No, thanks, not for me! I know what trying to make a career in a hospital is like, I've lived through it, and run away from it.

Besides, in that kind of a setup, you need a back that can bend, and mine is too Corsican for me to put up with much.

Or to hop into the sack readily either.

For several years my life was like a desert. I had buried Vanina deep within me, under sand dunes, but while my body was able to live, to vibrate, to reach a climax, my heart was still dead, a petrified muscle that no other woman was able to make beat.

Only eight years later, when Laurence came along, did I taste what happiness was like again.

At twenty-two, I decided I'd make love with a man.

I was neither prudish nor naïve, never the last to laugh at our stupid little medical-school dirty jokes, or, during dissections, to play some of the ghoulish farces that get passed on from generation to generation (like detach the penis from the cadaver and slip it into the coat pocket of the most stuck-up girl student), no fewer today than when all the students were men.

I decided I would sleep with a fellow because I really was curious to know what kind of sensations you could get from it. He was a pharmacy student. He had been most devoted in the way he courted me; I didn't go to bed with him feeling as if I were going to the slaughterhouse or the operating table. I approached heterosexual love without any prejudice, without disgust, mistrust, or disenchantment, but with the greatest goodwill—it seemed a very natural thing.

He did everything he could to make me appreciate the sex act. He was not bad at kissing, and caressed well, and knew how to use his member without haste or precipitation, thoughtfully, making every effort to please me.

But I got nothing. Neither pleasure nor displeasure. It was just a nice little game of legs in the air that was about as satisfying as eating a good meal or seeing a good film.

We went at it again several more times. I tried playing an active part. But petting his thing didn't do anything for me one way or the other. I liked it much better when he petted mine or when he took me. He was very unhappy about it all, but full of courage. "I want to make you come," he panted.

If there had been such a thing, while he went to work

on me, he would have kept his eyes on the instructions in the pages of the *Handbook for Bringing About an Orgasm in the Very Willing Woman Who Seems to Stall Halfway Through.*

I fought for it all the way, with him and with seven other men, too. Men of every stripe and hue, some young and some not so young, some just good-looking and some smart, some boors and some perfect gentlemen. In each case, we ended up good friends, once they gave up trying to give me that little something extra that makes all the difference. Even now, I have men friends who ask me why I won't marry them. Not because they want to make love to me, but out of friendship, out of caring, because perhaps they find in me an openness, a comprehensiveness that the other women they meet don't have. Obviously, I'm not the least bit interested; and, while I turn down all of their proposals on that score, I maintain a fine relationship of intellectual friendliness with them. I think what it is that won't work between men and me is that I need that extra dimension they don't have—communication, of which I have found only the negative aspect, that is, the No they say to that natural disposition toward universality which is the quality of women.

Woman can take on her virile dimension much better than man can let out the feminine part of himself. And that is what is *necessary* in order to achieve true fulfillment.

And besides, Woman is Beauty, Woman is Sensuality, two attributes so rarely to be found in man.

Let me say that there are certain intellectual attitudes in men against which I react most violently. But that I do so as woman and *feminist*, not as woman and *lesbian*.

For example, when they claim that the only women who are lesbians are the ones who can't get themselves fucked, I answer as a feminist that to a man a hole is a hole, and since he can slip his rod into a warm-water-filled rubber vagina or a cactus leaf that has been split in two, unattractive women have just as good a chance of getting themselves deflowered or violated as B.B. or M.M., and that there are no more lesbians who are homely and therefore unable-to-get-fucked than there are fruitful mothers so ugly they make you wonder how anyone ever got it up for them.

Besides, homeliness is something you have to live with, it's not something of your own doing; but vulgarity is of one's own doing.

How does one define vulgarity, the vulgarity of heart and action? (Vulgarity of speech and words is something quite different.)

Is *cock* in itself a vulgar word, or is it vulgar only because it is always used with filth either on the tip of one's tongue or pen?

I'm for outright frankness in words. And if I whisper or cry out to a woman, as we are making love, "I'm coming!" I tear the word away from the pages of pornographic books, from the leers of bawdy songs, and it sings in us and for us.

Eight men, eight years . . . Until Laurence came along, as I said; and, beginning with her, my heart was beating again, I could sweep away those diversion-men, those cover-up lovers with whom I had been sprinkling my feminine affairs.

For I was still making love to woman in the person of randomly met women. In that, too, you might say, I was being heterogeneous more than heterosexual. I didn't have, and still don't have, any one specific type of woman that appeals to me. The same, I believe, goes for most women.

I've had a lot of good men friends who, having gotten divorced from some ballbreaker or a small tub of lard, inevitably made a second marriage to another pain in the ass or another Miss Five-by-Five, as if each man remained faithful to a certain conception of woman.

Maybe we girls are more fanciful, allowing our eyes and our hearts to gambol over all kinds of new and therefore unpredictable paths . . .

In a word, just like the young she-goats of my native maquis, I grazed at ten different bushes, inhaling ten aromas, and, goatlike, ran away when I felt the other was trying to or going to become permanent. Why was it Laurence rather than another who restored my desire to live with a woman and make love over and over again without surfeit? Her body was covered with a very fine down, from the shoulders to the hollow of the thighs. Ardent and eager, at twenty-five she was just discovering women and their lovemaking.

She moved in with Laetitia and me, in the little studio apartment we now had on Rue Dragon.

Laetitia was still there with me; we were faithful sisters, a two-part family, one solid block, a couple that could not be dissolved.

Laetitia was the one everyone thought was the lesbian when we went out together; and, of course, it was taken for granted that we were "together." Her face is squarer than mine, her hair is cut shorter, and she wore slacks, to add to the confusion—which is enough for most people, for whom the clothes make the man just as the opportunity makes the thief.

Oh, Laetitia! My more-than-sister! Our love has nothing incestuous about it, there was never the slightest suggestion of troubled emotions between us, yet incestuous we are nonetheless . . . Our relationship is unique, being so intense, so solid. I've never had the same kind with anyone else, nor she with anyone but me. Every glance, every silence become a medium of communication with us, that's how attuned we are to each other emotionally, intellectually, and spiritually.

To me, Laetitia always represented weakness, which I had to defend and support. When we were kids, and my father's storms broke out, it was into my hand that she slipped hers, so that together, united, we endured both the shouting and the laughter. We are jealous and attentive to everything that affects the other. We are exclusionists, for having struggled so hard together to make our determination come true, to get away from our inherited peasantry, we share all of our mutual past as well as our mutual potential.

And now we had pulled it off together. I was a physician, and Laetitia was teaching math.

For a long time she had disapproved of my inversion.

She had been upset and concerned when she discovered it, and shocked as well. It must be said that the circumstances under which she learned of my homosexuality were not the most favorable. In Marseilles, when we lived together, and shared the same bed, there was a terrible rainstorm one night. My lover of the moment had come to our place for dinner. I didn't want her to go out on a night like that, and I urged her to stay with us. And so to bed, the three of us, me between the other two. And then—

Well, I thought Laetitia had fallen asleep—but she hadn't.

To her, this discovery came almost as a breakup, for inside her, I won't say in her unconscious but in her very depths, I was the one she would have wanted to have her first sex with. She would have liked me to introduce her to sex as I had introduced her to culture.

And she was hurt by it, for a long time. She would attack my girl friends, systematically run them down, making awful scenes to me that left my lovers perplexed and wondering.

But if she was jealous of my women, she never was of any of the men who went through my life.

She finally got herself a boyfriend, a very nice, sweet fellow, very well mannered; then another one, whom she pushed around, acting dictatorial, capricious, and sharp, while assuring me she was wonderfully happy as one could be only with a man, she in whom the "true faith" resided; but all of these things were said and done only to provoke me.

Then Laetitia went to Martinique as a teacher for two years. Two years away from me. And while she was there she experienced her first woman . . .

Being far away from me, the only way she could get closer was by identifying with me. Then in one of her pupils, who was aggressive and always trying to provoke her, she recognized herself. She recognized her own hostility toward the women who surrounded me. She recognized the unrequited, muted love against which she had been struggling without ever knowing it. Laetitia shed her respectability and threw herself into inversion with a glorious exaltation that amazed me when I saw her again, on her return to France.

Thereafter, nothing more separated us at all. We were sisters even in our lovemaking. In our hearts as in our thoughts, man had become obsolete. Laetitia, who had always been so unreceptive to my girl friends, consequently welcomed Laurence, who happened to come on the scene just after her discovery of the Holy Grail.

I was finishing my medical studies. With my thesis done, my specialization behind me, I spent a year filling in for others, and then went into practice for myself.

Talk about being down on your uppers! For a while I hadn't had any real financial worries, but now they came in full force. Fortunately, Laurence earned monthly wages that were paid regularly. But once again, I needed the wiliness of Sitting Bull, and every other trick and dodge I had used so much in the past, to delay a payment, turn away a creditor. Two tough years of trying to make ends meet. But then my practice picked up, I started working around the clock, and my tiny brick-colored car held up until I could afford to replace it with a better one.

After three years in Marseilles, I decided it was time to make my move up to Paris, because I was wasting away in the intellectual wasteland of the provinces. Laurence went with me.

That was fourteen years ago.

My work? Wonderful.

Life? Beautiful.

Love? We have an unforced faithfulness, an immense tenderness for each other, and no yen at all for one-night stands. We are a couple, accepted as such by our friends—and as for those who don't so accept us, they can go fuck themselves, plain and simple.

I have no desire and indeed no *time* to run after the odd passing woman.

And Lord knows how many of them pass through my office. I chose to specialize in gynecology because, loving women as I do, I wanted to be of help to them, to be able to assist them in their problems, ease their pains. I don't think any male practitioner, however great his talent and qualities, can approach and understand the problems and illnesses of a woman the way I can approach them myself. If I did opt for gynecology, it is also in part because I know I don't empathize with the psychology of the male, whereas between my woman patients and me there is a complicity, a similarity of vocabulary and an identity of gesture that make me much more "operative" than a male doctor of equal accomplishment.

Gynecology is mostly in the hands of men, and they decide to remove a woman's uterus more offhandedly than they would pull a tooth; for a tooth is at least useful for eating . . . Does every man who gets a cyst on his spermatic cord have one of his testes cut off?

But the male gynecologist can't realize, can't "understand" from within, the endocrine, and even more especially psychic, upsets that are caused by a hysterectomy, which any woman who hasn't been properly prepared, sufficiently conditioned for it feels to be a real amputation.

And who can describe how different it is to get a vaginal examination from a man, who sinks his fingers blindly, unfeelingly into the cavity that has only clinical meaning for him, unable to sense how such a brutal penetration may seem like a veritable rape to the woman lying there, legs spread, her feet in the stirrups of the examining table, in a position which of itself is at the least embarrassing, if not outright humiliating?

More and more, women are choosing to go to women gynecologists, and not out of any kind of sexism, but just out of pure logic.

I'm forty-five years old. I'm very well satisfied with life, not too badly preserved, but in two or three years I'll have a facelift. There's an operation that hasn't yet been accepted as part of French life! Those who have it done, hide it as if they had had some shameful disease. Yet age and its ravages are no disease, just one of the inevitable facts of life we have to take into account. You can live with wrinkles and bags under your eyes, you can accept your face in which time has dug its furrows, traced its ravines, but you can also, and most legitimately, reject the collapse of your flesh, and try to counteract the flaccidity of your skin without thereby becoming "an old bag who got it pulled back," in the horrible expression that men have coined and their women taken over.

I don't actually have any overly great fondness for youth. I am not attracted by the flowers within the budding grove, because for me love is more a mutual exchange of bodies and minds than a one-way gift, the one giving her tender, firm body while the other brings to it her culture and experience of life. But that does not shock me either. I am much less embarrassed by two women one of whom might be the other's mother than I am by an old graybeard who robs the cradle.

Why are people so much more tolerant of December-May couples like that, when they're ready to sneer at elderly ladies who find themselves young lovers?

A rheumatic spermatozoon with a long white beard thinks it's perfectly natural for its little tail to go knocking at the door of an eighteen-year-old ovary.

But a sixty-year-old woman with infertile ovaries is not supposed to have any right to a lusty graceful young lad.

It seems to be less shocking for the little sex kitten to be seen with the dirty old man than for the shameless old lady to want a young tomcat. Why? Remember, old Job could find warmth between two virgins, while old Rachel was left to crouch in manure. Accepted as perfectly normal. It's just a question of productivity.

I love making love, but that is not the essential part of my love relationships. To go to the theater together and laugh or exclaim over the same things, to go away on vacations together, side by side to read in silence the books one enjoys—these all are also ways of making love. Sensitive women, sensual women, intellectual women, women who may be willing partners, or contrary ones, or accomplices —I have loved them all in my own secret and reserved fashion, with a head that they sometimes said was too cool, but a warm heart and body. You daughters of Eve and Adam are so "lateralized," because people have unswervingly insisted that the costal area of a man's ribs gave "birth" to you . . .

One morning, shortly after I awakened, while the cleaning woman was bringing me my tea in bed, an idea suddenly came to me, for no particular reason, having no apparent connection with the news I was distractedly glancing at in the morning paper. I said to myself: "Enough of Adam's rib. Or else, if we do accept it, then Adam must be my grandmother."

Let me explain.

Adam has to be my ancestress, because that ridiculous

story of God taking one of his ribs is the normal conclusion and the incontrovertible proof of the male maternity fantasy.

"And Adam gave birth to Eve, and they had many children."

Now just a minute! The Lord formed man "of the dust of the ground," but then what did he form woman of? Bone? Can it be that we are made of more noble stuff? . . . That we are therefore superior to man and of higher quality?

Oh, no, not at all! Remember, it wasn't a *woman* who wrote the Bible. That glossary was accumulated by *men*, so they weren't paying us any compliments. They were making us *dependent* on man, just simply because we had been *born of* him. "Thank you, Adam, for having sacrificed a little bit of yourself for me to be knocked together from. I could exist only in *function* of you, *thanks* to you, *for* you, since I am *of* you, and since I owe you my existence, I owe you ALL. Thank you, Adam."

No, enough of that. If I was born of Adam's rib, then Adam is my grandmother, and one is not dependent on a granny. And there is no reason for my old gran to hold the distaff all by herself and be the only one to hold the reins and drive the phaeton!

Ah, men! On what analyst's couch will they ever divulge their maternity fantasy? Because they all have it, deeply rooted within them. And that frustration of theirs must certainly be powerful, for them to have erected our entire civilization on so ludicrous a postulate!

One might reasonably expect that a God so rational (despite a few aberrations that sometimes make you wonder whether the Great Clockmaker in the Sky wasn't just a bungling tinkerer), having foreseen everything, planned it all, would right from the start create He both a man *and* a woman.

But, no, oh, no! Man alone was enough. After all, he

was perfection (in His image). It was only a little later, after that first Sunday, say maybe by the following Wednesday or Thursday, that He bethought Himself to change His mind and create a woman to "keep Adam company," the way you add an olive to a Martini once it's mixed.

Company for man, she was to be, just as the dog is his best friend, so that from the very first woman was fated to have a secondary place.

But when He set about compensating for his omission, God did not form woman *ex nihilo* or from common clay, but out of Adam's rib, which is another way of saying his *uterus*. There is the male maternity fantasy made concrete, and nothing can make me see it otherwise.

The whole Adam myth can be thrown away. The female sex apparatus is the basic model, while the male sex organ is just a knockup of "added pieces." Until the fiftieth day of embryonic life, the structure is identical in all embryos, whether they are genetically male or genetically female. And, failing the presence of masculinizing factors (testosterone, most of all), the female form is the one that develops.

In other words, Genesis ought to be rewritten in the light of modern biological knowledge, and it ought to read: "And God created something that turned out to be the feminine potential, and then, realizing that it would not be good for woman to be alone, injected He some Y chromosome so as to give birth to man." And in that way, the "second sex" would in fact become the first, biologically speaking.

We were had right from that very first Wednesday or Thursday after Creation by the one who for two thousand years was going to relegate us to caves, to harems, to the women's quarters, to convents and kitchens.

We let ourselves be cowed for centuries and tens of centuries by the one who had enough muscle to drag the dinosaur around by its tail, to swing the deadly clubs, and wear heavy armor. But where does that affirmative virility get to express itself today except in pressing down on the gas pedal or pushing the lawn mower?

Not too long ago, on a plane trip, I happened to be seated next to a male psychoanalyst.

We had a delightful conversation—and I don't think the poor man ever got over it!

After I had given him a good dose of my viewpoint about that old rib-chop tale, I asked him a question which had been bothering me for quite a while: Had he noted, in the last few years, any change in the attitude and behavior of his women patients, after all the noise that had been made by the feminist movements, the campaigns for legalizing the pill, for abortion, against rape, and so on?

No, he couldn't say that he had . . .

"Well, none so deaf as those who will not hear," I told him. "You don't see any change in them because you don't *want* to see any. So you turn it off. Quite unconsciously, you put a quietus over their subconscious and even their conscious. You have no right to do that, and you can't do any valid analyses in 1978 if you go at them just the way you did in 1960."

Someone, I don't remember who, said: "Men call vices those pleasures that elude them, and virtues, the infirmities that stay with them."

Let them beware of the virtuous women who remain at their sides, they may not always be so infirm. They may yet have legs enough to run and throw themselves into our arms if men don't decide to treat them differently, no longer to treat them as vassals, but rather as equals, messmates: "those who eat at the same table" with their lord and master, the lord whose bed they have shared since the dark night of the beginning of time; now the least they want is to share his life as well.

So beware, men. Drop some of your ballast. Loosen the reins, lest one day your overburdened she-ass, your over-bridled mare, your boxed-in female finally raise her head and bite you in the crotch, or in the heart.

Well, I guess I've used up my second.

"A Second for Lesbians," if you don't mind . . .

BEIJA FLOR

If it was tough to be a lesbian in 1938, how does it feel to be one in 1978? In forty years, what barriers have fallen away, what prejudices have disappeared, what windows have been opened?

I live amid much too much excitement, much too close to the heart of the stream, surrounded now by young girls as ever I have been, to be able properly to measure the difference. I can't really feel it, just as we do not see people grow older when they are beside us day after day. I had to back off at some distance, stop bathing in the river, climb back up on the bank, and, sitting on a rock, look upstream and then downstream, in order to get some view of what those forty years had brought by way of change or lack of it.

Have things really changed very much? Is today's young lesbian at twenty-five much different from what I was at her age? Have all mothers now become as tolerant as my own, have civil services dropped the seal of shame that used to preclude any advancement, have men decided to put down their weapons, and have women gotten to talk about us without that embarrassment that sounds all too much like fear?

I was anxious to find out.

It was luck that led me to the one who could reveal to me how you live out the fact of your lesbianism at twenty in 1978.

Beija flor is the name that Brazilians give to the hummingbird, a poetical name: *beija flor*, kiss-the-flower . . . A tiny bird so unbelievably delicate it seems to have been created by the brush of a Japanese painter. Its lines are clean and short, precise and wiry, a tiny bird whose wings beat and throb at a pace so unbelievable that they become invisible. Its beak is sharp as a stiletto as it plunges into the depth of the pistils to drink up their dew. *Beija flor*, bird-beauty quenching its thirst at the flower-beauty.

Athirst for flower-women, beautiful and delicately built, tiny and tough, haughty and tender, my own Beija Flor has the name of Catherine.

I met her at Cannes, in the month of August.

I had gone down to the Midi to do the "book-signing bit." La Croisette was hot, pulsating, throbbing with people, the Café du Festival had its terrace overflowing with dazzling tanned beauties. On my way up to the drug store, my eyes glancingly caught sight of a ravishing little Vietnamese girl sitting alone at a table, paying a quick tribute to her, giving me a quick free lift. With her golden skin, her coal-black slanted eyes, raven hair down to her hips, she had that Asian grace peculiar to Balinese dancers or Cambodian apsaras. My admiring eyes lingered briefly on her, while I regretfully thought, for, alas! it is all too often true: She's too *feminine* to be a lesbian. Too bad! Meantime, her eyes had passed indifferently over me. And why not? What did I expect? What can I look like to that ravishing Tanagra? A mature lady who's not even suntanned, going into the drug store like some tourist to pick up a luxury fashion magazine . . .

They made a place for me, seated behind a table, between piles of books, and I waited for the customers to appear. With amusement, out of the corner of my eye, I watched the woman dawdling between aisles, riffling through a book here and there, moving away, coming nearer, hesitating, timid, slightly ashamed. She was a silver trout, moving in to sniff at my bait, then drawing away as I tried to reel her in. Would she dare to do it, dare to come near me, the "public lesbian"? There's an odor of sulfur about me. I'm on fire—and anyone who comes near is making known her solidarity, falling in line under my banner, and immediately branded . . . That one kept turning and turning, the longest time, and then gave up and left, with a book she picked up at random. Next time, madame, don't be afraid, don't be ashamed. Just because you buy a lesbian's book, the shelves won't explode around you, people won't start laughing at you, and I won't gobble you up, pink though you be, or slap you on the shoulder, yelling, "Comrade lesbian!" The only reason you're ashamed is that you feel involved in it.

Well, there was one who was willing. Her face drawn tight, she circumspectly shoved a copy of the book toward me for me to sign, as if I were giving her a passport to some other life, or a prescription to treat what bothered her. I smiled at her, but not too broadly. She seemed too much on edge. If I acted too cordial she'd have taken fright. But it was a step in the right direction. She dared. Tomorrow, perhaps, her daring would go on to other things. Like not staying in the closet anymore, no longer being ashamed of her loves, getting up the courage to touch the hand, the heart, and finally the sex of another woman. Very well, madame, you've done all right, and now keep it up. You've broken through the first hoop, and you can smash the next ones, turn into a roaring lioness, a catlike panther, a royal tigress; go on and accept your lesbianism, let yourself bloom, shake out your petals, open your corollas . . .

"For Mademoiselle So-and-so, very sincerely . . ."

I raised my eyes, and there was my little Tanagra coming into the bookstore. She came up to me without the slightest hesitation, quite composed. She held out a book to me that she had brought in her handbag, and said, "My name is Catherine."

I was delighted that so pretty a creature should be interested in us. Yes, she was originally Vietnamese, but she had known nothing of the country of the yellow balilas.

Her parents, who were naturalized French, had left Saigon when she was just two months old, sailing off in 1955 toward a mother country they had never seen before. She doesn't even speak Vietnamese. Yet, she is Asian down to the tips of her long little fingers, to her slightly flattish nose, her high cheekbones, right to the end of her tiny body, her narrow, round hips, her breasts, those sweet guavas, and her hibiscus-red mouth.

She lived in Nice, and as it happened I was going to be going there after dinner, for another autographing session, at my friend Gisou Gardoni's new club. So I suggested that I might take her back. In order to get to Cannes and see me, she had had to take a train, and then a bus.

We went out to dinner together. I listened to her intently. I was dazzled. Everything that this twenty-three-year-old little Beija Flor of mine was telling me, in her ardor, her violence, her refusals to compromise, her excesses, her tendernesses, hopes, and conceptions, all were the things I would have wished to be able to put into words myself at her age. Minute my minute, she grew closer and closer to me.

What I was hearing was an echo of myself, at a twenty-five-year remove, a belated picture of what I would have liked to be. I am envious of Beija Flor, because she has always known what she was, because she never let a man have sway over her body, because she never let herself be stabbed by a penis and never would.

Beija Flor is built. She's solid as a rock. Stubborn, violent, aggressive, she can talk aloud about her homosexuality, shout it out if she wants, because she has every right. She sees the society we live in and the conditions that are set for us with the eyes of a twenty-three-year-old girl. My own eyes are somewhat worn. I no longer so clearly see the bare bones, my heart and my blood may beat a little less quickly than they did once, and I no longer have exactly the same notion of love and relationships between women, between women and men, between Woman and Man.

Beija Flor speaks to me in a vocabulary of revolt that attracts and rejuvenates me. She speaks in the future tense, whereas I am beginning to be most familiar with the past. I listen to her, take a good look at how she lives, and it's like a fountain of youth. I am sorry that I'm no longer her age, that I no longer am capable of that degree of violence, which once was mine, too, and which it moves me so to recognize again in her.

She still lives in Nice. From time to time she gets to come to Paris, to see me at home. It is all just as natural as can be, as if she had always been a member of my family.

She is a gulp of cool water, she is singing crystal, she is vibrant beauty, she is the love of love. Flower-girl, bird-girl, that's Beija Flor.

And here is the story she has to tell.

* * *

As far back as I can remember, I've never loved anyone but women; yet I had to meet Annick to find out what sex was all about. It was at Dakar, where my father was working at the time.

She came into the bistro near the lycée, where we used to hang out after school.

I was immediately attracted to her. She was tall, with green eyes, and a curly Afro haircut. She looked like a saucy young boy, with awkward gestures, but a calm, warm, deliberate voice. She was twenty-two.

When she put her arm around my waist, I was turned on, and didn't try to stop her. She looked me in the eyes, bent over me, placed her lips on mine for a moment that seemed like an eternity to me. And then her tongue slipped in, like a warm petal, sweet-soft, feeling out my own.

Within me I felt a sensation of warmth, a terribly strong one, that went right down into my vagina. Never had I felt anything like it.

"My folks are away," she said. "Come up to my place." We walked back there. She lived up on the *corniche*. No one was on the streets at that hour of the night. Dakar belonged to us and protected us. Annick led the way, with her arm around my shoulders. From time to time, we would stop and kiss one another. The sky was exploding with stars, the sea was breaking at our feet; it was almost warm.

She poured me a drink and then kissed me some more. I felt her fingers opening my blouse. She was undressing me, slowly, her hands moving softly over my breasts, her lips lingering on my neck. I was tingling with pleasure. Then I in turn undressed her, and once we were nude she stretched out on top of me.

I felt her cunt against mine, and the same warmth as that of the first kiss spread all through me again.

Her skin was soft, her hand went down and then came up the length of my body with exasperating slowness. Her lips had taken my lips, then my breasts, then my belly, and had come, finally, to rest on my cunt.

She kissed it slowly, softly, until I had the feeling that I simply didn't exist anymore. Pleasure had submerged me. I was sixteen years old and it was dazzling to discover what a climax could be.

Then it was my turn to make love to her. Probably ineptly, but with an infinite amount of desire. She had put her hand on my head and helped by guiding me. I kissed her slowly, long and deep, just the way she had done for me, and then I felt her tensing and rising. Her thighs locked themselves around my face. She was coming . . . Oh, God, how beautiful it was that she was coming that way!

Then I fell asleep, a long time later, with my head on her shoulder.

I was no longer a child. I had become a woman. I now

looked down on my friends at the lycée with a kind of condescension, wondering whether it could be that they would never know that happiness I had known.

We didn't get to make love often, because we both lived at home with our parents and had no place where we could go, but we made out a great deal. Anywhere and everywhere. Without the slightest inhibition. People didn't point their fingers at us—that's not the way it's done in Africa—but their tongues were wagging plenty. I couldn't have cared less. I was happy, and I sure didn't want to make a secret of it. But not because I was trying to provoke them. I was only sixteen, and I thought people were intelligent enough to understand that happiness is not a question of sex but a question of love.

I didn't know anything about homosexuality. It had just happened that I had made love with a *woman*, which didn't bother me in the slightest, since I was in love with her. To me there was no problem, no question, no worry, no hesitation. I loved Annick and it so happened that Annick was a woman, just as it happened that my heart had never beat for anyone but women, as it happened that my eyes had never admired anyone but women. What was wrong with that?

That was the year that Papa died, a very quiet death, like an oil lamp flickering out, taking time to smile to each of us first, one by one; the months that followed I lived in total unreality. It wasn't my father who had died, it wasn't my mother who was weeping, and we weren't the ones living through this. The house had no more soul, and the family no longer existed. We went back to France, where I began to study law at Nice. But my heart wasn't in it. I didn't laugh anymore. I didn't cry anymore. I just let myself go to a somber lethargy that wiped out any emotions I might have. I accepted life, but without actually living it.

That went on that way for a year, and then I felt as though I had awakened from a very long, dreamless sleep.

Because I was eighteen at the time, and at eighteen no one really wants to die.

I started going out again. I used to go to a wide-open joint, where sometimes two women would dance together. I felt at ease there, and seeing them like that warmed my heart.

My mother, who sometimes went there with me, would look at those women with an eye that was half-shocked, half-curious. She had no idea that her daughter was a lesbian. But at the time who could have suspected it? I talked with the men there, danced with them, and so to her I looked just like a "normal" girl, until the day when, having drunk a bit too much, I started coming on to a woman on the dance floor.

My mother didn't say anything about it. But the next day, when I told her I was going out, she absolutely forbade me to go there.

It was as if she were asking me to forswear my homosexuality!

We had an argument about that—as short as it was violent. My brother tried to block the door. I threw myself upon him. I was not going to give in. I was not going to agree not **to** go out! Not because this particular time mattered, but because I knew that if I gave in now, I would have to give in for all the rest of my life and that I would spend it all in darkness and shame. That was something I would not put up with. I am among those who prefer light to darkness. No one was going to stand in the way of my following my natural bent.

It was my life, as I understood it, not the way the rest of them envisioned it, my own true life that was at stake. It meant either to go on living with the truth or else to go on living with a perpetual lie. These thoughts gave me the strength of ten. I fought so hard that I finally slipped right through my brother's arms and got away. My mother, behind me, had broken into tears. My brother was wild and yelled out that I was "abnormal," that I was a "dirty pervert."

That break was inevitable. I never could have kept my homosexuality forever quiet, even if the truth of it had to hurt those who were close to me. Papa's death had taught me at least one thing: Life is too short for anyone to live it according to other people's rules.

That night I went on the biggest drunk of my life. I slept with the first girl I found and then another, and another, and didn't get home till three days later. When I saw how resigned the family was, I knew I had won the fight. I would finally be able to live my life out in the open.

But it was a long, hard struggle. Not any pitched battle, but a sullen, endless, undermining campaign. How I had to shut myself off so as not to be influenced by all the "good advice" I was always getting!

I turned a deaf ear to the siren songs that hinted how easy things could be if I just got myself a "nice, understanding" husband. Why should I have "slept with a man to find out whether I was really a lesbian" when I knew damned well that I was? I find it hard to comprehend that sort of reasoning . . .

I am one of those who can't even *think about* making love with a man. I am physically repelled by their physical shape, by what Benoîte Groult in her book describes in words something like "That thing that hangs limp so much more often than it displays its stuff . . ." Even if one day I were to fall in love with a man, at best it would only be a platonic friendship, because I could never get over that physical hump. It takes more of an escalation than I can countenance.

* * *

That was when she met Nathalie.

Up until then, whether in clubs or restaurants, all she had met were "polyvalent" women, and such rare lesbians as she came across were usually ready to be accommodating to any easy mark, provided there was enough cash in it to help them eke out their tight month's-end expenses.

That was the atmosphere in which she was "learning." But Beija Flor, my pure and uncompromising little sister, was one who could dance in the mud without being spattered. Sometimes a flower would bloom where Beija Flor had been.

Nathalie, an air stewardess, noticed Beija Flor during a stopover, at a club in Haut-de-Cagnes, and took her back to the hotel on the Promenade des Anglais in Nice where her crew was billeted.

She was thirty-eight. And a beauty. Not the stereotypical beauty that most twenty-year-olds are, all so similar in their budding allure, but a beauty that has been developed and sculpted by life. The beauty of a real woman-woman.

Lying on the bed, Nathalie gazed at Beija Flor undressing. That look, far from embarrassing the girl, appealed to the exhibitionistic side of her character. She was beautiful and well aware of it.

She slipped out of her skintight jeans with the nonchalant gracefulness of a water serpent, and quickly ducked out of her tailored shirt, so many buttons of which had already been open anyway, and she emerged nude, with the harmonious dip of the small of her back, that soft, sinuous, matte, and golden line blending into narrow but round hips, hard, high buttocks, perfect globes, her thick, black, almost blue Asian hair twisting like a waterfall down her arching back.

And arching as much as she could so as not to lose an inch of her small height, she turned toward Nathalie, lying, silently watching, on the bed. Her breasts came as a surprise on that slim little body. Round, aggressive, in full bloom, their tiny little girl's tips surrounded by a pale circle, scarcely a pinkish shadow.

And moved toward the bed. Nathalie took her face between her hands, kissed her almost gently, and got up.

She got undressed in her turn, simply, naturally. Naked, she was even more beautiful than before. Time had as yet in no way ravaged her. At most, her chest was perhaps a little less aggressive, her belly a mite less hard and flat.

A wave of moving emotion came over Beija Flor. For the first time in her life, she was gazing upon a nude woman, a real woman in the prime of her beauty, her sensuality, a statue of full-blown flesh.

They came into each other's arms violently, for each desired the other with a fierce animal desire.

Nathalie was gifted with the femininity, the sensuality, the lasciviousness of women who love being able to cause the pleasure of love and love equally to receive it. Her hand, with consummate skill, contained Beija Flor's pleasure while they devoured each other's lips like cannibal flowers, the gossamer threads of their merging saliva still holding them joined when Nathalie raised her head to admire that young face thrown back, in abandon, eyes closed, all converging on a tiny spot of her body, a spot so fragile, so delicate and yet so powerful, so omnipotent, so essential, so sovereign.

Sweet torture. Slowness of the approach. Finally, her lips against that cunt that was calling to her. Beija Flor was giving herself entirely to what she nevertheless knew had to be a one-night stand without follow-up. But Nathalie was love. There was no sort of inhibition in her. Nothing was off limits. She gave and gave of herself without any restraint whatever. She experienced an almost animal pleasure, a pure pleasure. . . .

Beija Flor was all wondrous on awakening in the arms of a woman whom only yesterday she had never heard of and whose skin this morning adhered so wonderfully to hers. Once again, their bellies met, their arms went around each other, their mouths possessed each other, and their cunts, those burning bushes, those lips of fire, rubbed against each other. Their short breaths sang into their ears, adding further to their ardor, to their heat, to their moistness and their sweetness.

In a hot and humid kiss they were joined one to the other, their legs intertwined. The dark fleece and the lighter one, undergrowths striated with rays of the sun, dewdrops forming like tears on the edge of eyelashes, shining streaks along the soft skin of the trembling thighs. Their hips began to sway, in a slow, regular rhythm, nothing like the ramming home of stallions, but the harmonious gait of two mares going from one end of the meadow to the other, quiet, their eyes half-closed, their manes waving, their nostrils atremble.

Nathalie slipped her hand along Beija Flor's body. Slowly, as if feeling her way, her sensitive fingertips reconnoitering the round shoulder, the breast with its tiny tip erect, the hollow of the hip, the thigh with its muscles hardened by exertion. Now she had to break the closeness of their two bodies, slip her hand in between them, penetrate into the tight warmth accumulated between their bellies, go on down to their cunts, work her way in and penetrate softly into Beija Flor's body, slide into the narrow passage with its velvet softnesses, and caress its satiny walls until she heard her song grow louder, her lament grow larger, and her groan finally explode into a cry.

Beija Flor was accessible, receptive, a female rolled about in a torrent of caresses such as had never been before. Woman, woman, what a wonderful thing a woman, how could one desire anything other than the love of a woman? . . .

At the end of that same summer she met Valérie.

Now on vacation on the Riviera, in Paris she was the kept friend of one of Mme. Claude's girls. These hetaerae, the most beautiful of all Paris, super-luxury prostitutes, all distinguished by their refined and never blatant beauty, who would be hard to tell from anyone else at an alumnae reunion of the Convent of the Birds, were often lesbians, as are so many of their consoeurs of the "lower orders."

How easy that is to understand, when they have to submit over and over again, whether for ten or a hundred thousand francs, to the same male buyer, some horse trader in a hurry to finish his deal, some consumer in a rush to complete his consummation. Once out of the Rolls-Royce or the VW, when the silk muffler or the greasy workingman's cap has been thrown onto the dresser, all you have is a man who's buying a woman who's selling.

Selling with indifference, oftentimes with disgust, and sometimes even hatred, always with disdain, a body that, as so many yogis have, they have learned to "disincarnate," to lend to the performance without participating in it.

A great many prostitutes become lesbians out of a need for gentleness, for kindness, a thirst for different gestures, different words, and Valérie was neither pimp nor gigolo (again, two words that have no feminine form—this time, perhaps a very good sign!), but just a somewhat lazy girl who had found a girl friend with easy money and who therefore had no reason to knock herself out working. She made no mystery of where her income came from—a point in her favor as far as Beija Flor, with her horror of lies, was concerned. And she told me so.

* * *

I was in love with the way she could undress me with her eyes (Beija Flor told me), the way she had of desiring me, and the way she took me.

She was a primitive, uncivilized, but a born lover. She would make love to me any old place, any old time. In building hallways, elevators, bathing cabanas, cars, nightclub ladies' rooms, wide places in the rock, bushes, anywhere, between Monte Carlo and Cannes I came groaning against her everywhere. When her eyes rested on me with a certain light in them that I knew well, I began to melt, to let myself go, body and soul.

Valérie was like an animal. She would take me once with bestial violence, and then with infinite sweetness. But she was totally lacking in that quality that I so love in a woman: true gentleness. We made love all through that long summer.

Then I had to get back to school. I wasn't doing so well in my law courses, and there was nothing I was sufficiently interested in to keep me in Nice. Valérie was going to return to Paris; I couldn't give her up, the idea of no longer making love with her was driving me crazy.

But once in Paris, I discovered an entirely different Valérie, a Valérie with a horrible, selfish character, totally concerned with herself, vulgar—and, especially, cowardly. Sure, she liked me and was interested in me, but she was much more interested in hanging onto her meal ticket.

I would sleep at her studio until noon, but after that I had to leave the coast clear until eleven at night, so as to be sure her girl friend didn't surprise us. You know how I hate compromises. So I wandered around an unknown, foreign, hostile Paris, with the sordid seats of its stinking subway, the cold, wet benches of its public squares, the mad crowds in the department stores, and the film sat through three times over in the cheap little movie houses . . . Some beautiful *vie parisienne* that is! I had no money, no plans, no hopes. And I hardly even had Valérie anymore. All of my wonderful world, my delightful dreams were crumbling. I didn't want to go back to Nice, and was unwilling to admit that I had made a mistake.

Everything she did was superficial and what she loved best was putting on airs. She was proud of how discreetly she could pick up the tab when we went out with friends, but then afterward boasted about it so that she became ridiculous. And as soon as we were alone together, she became miserly and petty. I had to turn to a woman friend of my mother's to borrow three hundred francs so I could rent a cheap little room in the Fifteenth Arrondissement.

Valérie wasn't willing to help in any way. "Take care of it yourself," she'd say. "I never asked you to come along."

Once I had my own place where I could spend my days, it didn't make things any better. Valérie refused to go to work (she never had) and refused to give up the girl friend who was keeping her. What kind of a milieu was this that I had fallen into? Women who acted like pimps and thought they were Don Juan, girls who came from nowhere and lavishly laid out the easy money they made selling their ass, a whole miserable world of unsavory corner-cutting, of pitiful little swindles . . .

Six months. I stuck it out for six months. But whereas Valérie's earlier fiancées may have been masochists, I was not one to stand around and get slapped without hitting back. It was grotesque! I had the feeling I was living with a man!

I finally decided I'd go back to Nice. I had been deeply hurt in my heart as well as my self-respect. I had loved Valérie passionately, with all of my being. I had believed in her, with all my strength. And I had been wrong.

Valérie taught me a great deal. With her I went through some of the most beautiful moments—as well as some of the worst. She allowed me the discovery of the homosexual world in its petty, vulgar aspect; showed me, through the people she associated with, what hypocrisy, nastiness, envy, and lying were. Things I had never even been able to imagine.

Thanks to her, I am a little better equipped to face life. Thanks to her, I am a bit more distrustful of other people.

On the other hand, Valérie was the one who brought me to the full consciousness of my own homosexuality. I understood that it was necessary to be lesbian not only for oneself, but also in the eyes of others.

For that, I am grateful to her.

One thing is certain, and that is that I'll never be found in the bed of a man.

* * *

You are smiling and shrugging your shoulders. Beija Flor is only twenty-five, and she dares to make such an affirmation, such a decision, without knowing whether tomorrow there may not be a triumphant penis rising on her horizon. She is going to live with that sort of sword of Damocles suspended over her, petrified, immobilized, paralyzed in the web that she herself is weaving, which is nothing more than a substitute for the prejudices and rules she claims she is rejecting. A prisoner of other obligations, other promises—the ones she makes to herself.

Why are you so skeptical of it? Does doubting her make you feel surer of yourself?

* * *

Am I in a state of mortal sin (she asks), I who am a woman who loves and is loved by other women? In olden times, I might have been burned at the stake as a witch, for the salvation of my soul.

I'm a lesbian, and yet it is hard for me to keep from believing in God. Because I do believe in a God who created the heavens and the earth. A weakness? It may be. A need? Without any doubt.

And the truth to me is to live in harmony with myself without committing aggression against the world around me, which rejects me because I am different.

What I do know, at any rate, is that I want to make a success of my life as a lesbian and my life as a woman.

I have to have a stable love life, and yet, at the same time, I'd like to make love to all the lesbians on earth!

So what should I choose? A solid, quiet love, or multiple beautiful loves that do not last?

What I do know now is that I will never again despair, because I know that there are suns in the world.

I will have several loves. But I already know that no love is exactly like any other, and that I will come out of each heart, each woman, richer, stronger, and more ardent.

The love of women will be sap and blood to me, and all I will ever again live for is to feel them flooding into my veins and my soul.

Cry foul all you want, men, but you will never have the pleasure of begetting a child on me.

Denounce me, mothers, for I have no maternal instinct, nor do I have any ache to hold in my arms a bit of the flesh of my flesh.

Those who think they're going to see me dragging on from year to year, from lover to lover, full of remorse over some imaginary missed chance at being a mother, need not delude themselves: I am not afraid of solitude, even if it means that at the twilight of my life I will end up all alone.

And you, closet lesbians, may disavow me, too, for I am living now and forever without complexes or regrets.

MADELEINE
(Concluded)

or, "When we are dead,
our ashes will be together"

I had almost finished my manuscript, was almost done compiling the statements and confidences; I had seen Élodie for the last time at dinner, Dany at lunch, Vanina at her office, or had Frédérique on the phone to clear up one last point. My heart was beating in all directions, my mind at times was getting wild with all the different images that went through it. I felt that I was Beija Flor and dreamt of Judith's love on the shore of the lake. I was woman in her many incarnations, sometimes amazed, coming out of the clouds, recovering from their loves and their sorrows; I looked upon the woman I love as if she were an intruder, an alien. I was in the moist heat of Abidjan with Sylvie and on the windswept heath with Anne-Marie. My eyes rose from the paper, going beyond the desk and the lamp, that privileged islet, that magic circle, where I was listening to all those lives and loves, and what they saw was the everydayness of a love that happened to be my own, which I had forgotten, neglected perhaps, for a few moments.

I was hesitant about how well justified some of my choices, some of my descriptions were: Were all these lives, all these thicknesses of existence that I had brought together here representative of a world that is mine? Would they allow the women who eventually read my book to grasp the simultaneously simple and complex reality that is our life? Would they be able to understand any better and to accept us?

I didn't know, but I hoped so.

And it was just then, when I was in that frame of mind, worried but at the same time exalted, that I had news of Madeleine. She was the one who had been the first in the ring with her loneliness and fragility. Now here she was, having gone back to the one love of her life, Lucienne. The latter was older than she, living her death agony. Madeleine had been unable to keep from going to her . . . There were two letters that told me about that meeting: They tell the end, or almost the end, of that story of the two Belgian nurses who loved each other in 1938.

* * *

Dear Elula,

. . . I just found out that Lucienne is very ill. You know, since the war, while we never completely lost sight of each other, we almost never got to see each other. At any rate, not alone. Never again alone together, never like it was back at the hospital . . . When her husband died, I had suggested to her that we move in together, inasmuch as I was now free to do so. She said No, on account of her mother, who had no one else to take care of her. That was ten years ago . . .

And today, I've found out that she is ill. Her heart—our hearts have grown old without each other . . . Tomorrow I'll try to get to Charleroi to see her. I want to get to talk to her, heart to heart for once, just one last time. Ask her the questions I never did ask her because, in our time, there were things you just didn't talk about. But there's always her sister there with her. I hope I'll be able to snatch her away for a couple of moments . . . I'll write you when I get back to tell you about it. I kiss you tenderly.

Madeleine

Dear Elula,

. . . I saw Lucienne. She appeared to me to have gotten much weaker, with a thin, almost emaciated face. It upset me terribly, but I didn't let on to her about it. I looked at her with the eyes of love. She is seventy years old. I so ardently desired to have her alone for myself for a few moments, no doubt because she is reaching the end of her life and I am beginning to know what that is like.

Oh, the miracle! At one point, her sister said she had to go out and run an errand! So I had to make it fast. I didn't know how to get started. Then, without any preamble, I told her that, throughout all my life, she had been the only true lover for me, the only one who ever gave me any real pleasure . . .

She was there across from me, sitting up in her bed, extremely tense. Then I could feel how she relaxed and I saw that light that I know so well shining in her eyes. I would have liked to kneel at her feet . . .

I asked her the question that has always haunted me:

"Had you been with any other woman before me?"

"No, you are the only one," she said. "I made a sensible marriage, too, you know, and every day was not a bed of roses."

She told me I oughtn't to have gotten married. "My mother would have taken care of your little girl," she said. But there had been my parents . . .

I told her she ought to have come to live with me when she was widowed, but then she had her mother.

"Now," I said to her, "that your mother is no longer here, we could still live together."

"I don't have the time for it, you know," she answered. "I'm not going to live much longer."

I broke out sobbing. I didn't want her to die. We went a long way during that half-hour tête-à-tête, the first one we had since 1941 . . .

Madeleine

We remembered all kinds of things. The night when the woman head of the nursing service came knocking at her door, and I had to go and hide under her bed. All those nights when we could never stay together until daybreak.

I told her about you. She told me that there were more women like us than people thought, but that she hoped that today's young girls would never be persecuted the way we were.

She asked me to have myself cremated, the way she was going to be. In the cemetery of her town there is a lawn where the ashes of cremated people are buried.

"If what you said is true," she said, "if I really was the only one you loved, leave instructions for that. That way, when we're dead our ashes will be together."

I've always been against cremation, but now I'll have to think about it. I'm the only one she loved, so how can I refuse her? For us to be together again in death, when our passion only lasted three years . . . Why did our life have to be so thwarted? Was it the price we had to pay for those three years of supreme happiness?

I would like to bring my tenderness, my presence to her. I told her so. I want to convince her we should still live together, in spite of her sister.

"You know, for me, physical love is all over. My heart wouldn't stand it anymore. How about you?" she asked me.

"Oh, I take pills to get away from the world, but I'd rather do it through love. My heart is young, it was put to so little use! But what I want most of all is to make you happy!"

I have the feeling that we love each other just as much as we did on the first day. I'll go back to Charleroi. I'll still try to talk her into it. I'm beginning to have hopes . . .

Madeleine

AND YOU

The circle is coming to a close: this landscape of women who prefer women, the heavy, gray clouds of Madeleine, Beija Flor's birdsong, the sorrows and passions, the hesitations and fears, the tenderness and the violence. Happy or unhappy, blooming flowers or flowers faded forever, they are my friends, my sisters . . .

These nine lives, or rather this one life with nine different voices which has just been sketched out, may make some feel that hopelessness, wild but unrequited desire, instability, occasional suffering, unavoidable difficulties are and will always be the fate of my sisters in lesbianism.

Who ever made the claim that we always lived in a valley of roses?

In order to experience the warmth of a body, the presence of the Other, that other woman we had not dared or not been able to touch, a breath, a hand, how many of us did—for a night, a month, or a year—take refuge with some man to whom we lent an inert body, an extinguished heart, a dried-up and much too lonely sex apparatus?

The permanent aggression of males—which conditions our entire lives since they rule them—forces us to make our way through a lifetime marked off by penises that we no longer love or never have loved at all. Are lesbians happy? Are these so-called perverse women satisfied in their skins? Can these allegedly vice-ridden creatures be blossoming, bursting with joy? Alas, no!

Our life is a narrow one, continually marred by obstacles. So how could we possibly blossom in a society that gags us, keeps us off to the side, sells us at the pornocrats' auction, points fingers at us? Those lesbians must be in a tiny minority who have had the good luck to have an understanding and open-minded husband or family, and a job in which homosexuality is not a handicap.

Yet, happy lesbians do certainly exist. They are the hidden part of the picture, of which I have so far scarcely sketched the outlines. At twenty, Ginette, a clerk in the French postal service in the small town of Romorantin, met Josette, who worked in a hardware store. That was thirty years ago, and they're still living together, still in Romorantin. There's nothing in that story to make a novel of, but it is quite enough to build a life upon.

Potential lesbians, lesbians at heart, are very numerous, perhaps much more numerous than the active lesbians. But many of those who know that they are, who are fully aware of their own true nature, will never gather up the courage to make the decisive crossing—to come out of the closet, as the current saying has it. Yet they know full well that their friends on the other side are waiting for them, calling to them. They watch us live, and love, and laugh, but they remain where they are on the shore of that oh! so delicious lake, which they will never dare dive into. These poor women have been chained down by the prejudices and taboos of a sexually unworthy society.

To have a homosexual daughter—what a horror! What a disgrace! What will people say?

We are not the ones who are scandalous—and anyway, where is the scandal? Only in the minds of others, in their fantasies, never in our own hearts. As for you, mothers, you need not worry, you've nothing to fear, homosexuality is not leprosy, and it is quite possible to be truly happy with a woman in one's heart and one's body; the only pain that you can legitimately feel, the only regret that is comprehensible to me, is that in that case perhaps your daughter will never favor you with grandchildren. And even on that score, how many of us are there (and increasingly as time goes on) who decide to have children, now that being a "bachelor mother" is no longer such a matter of scorn in the view of most people? (Or am I being too optimistic?)

We have looked into the lives of nine women. Be aware that you are undoubtedly the tenth. You who are a lesbian but are not aware of it, you who are not a lesbian and never will be.

Just try daring to say that you saw no trace of yourself in any of those women, that in none of those mirrors did there appear a reflection that seemed familiar to you. These strange and different sisters, these potential sisters, may well be very close to you—for you, too, are a woman.

Be aware that there is nothing for which you need forgive them, and nothing that you should hold against them. We are not monsters. We are your daughters, your sisters, and, yes, your mothers, too. The crimes of child rape, the butcheries, the mayhem, the little battered bodies shoved under the bed as if they were so much dust—these are never the work of women, no, ma'am. Not of those of you who love men, or of those of us who love women. For one Countess Bathory that comes along, how many Landrus, Bluebeards, Gilles de Rais, and Jack the Rippers are there?

The persecuted unwed mother who drowns her newborn infant, the gun-toting gangster girl, even the murderess never, or almost never, act out of an uncontrollable sexual impulse. Sex crimes are perpetrated by men. They wield their male organ as if it were a dagger, they invade our turfs, they trample on our bellies, and relieve themselves inside our bodies without ever asking whether we like it. "Sleep with me to make me happy" was what Dany's husband used to say to her. Well, no, no, and never again!

We women love, that is, we love a being or we love the fact and act of love, but we never just "naturally" impose our domination upon our fellow beings, and especially not on the being of our choice.

Don't be afraid of us, the rest of you who, without doubt, at some time in your lives have found your eyes meeting ours, welcomed our smiles, fleetingly shared a bit of complicity . . .

So you, madame, who are that tenth one, please, when you hear someone around you making fun of us, leering and sneering as they say, "She's a dyke," won't you answer:

"Yes, she *is* a lesbian. What difference does that make?"

Believe me, when you do, there will be an awful lot of us who will be silently sending our thanks to you.